Philippines: The Silenced Democracy

Philippines:
The Silenced Democracy

Raul S. Manglapus

ORBIS BOOKS
MARYKNOLL   NEW YORK

To my wife and sons,
who had the courage to escape
from the Marcos dictatorship
so that I might feel free
to speak my piece

CONTENTS

FOREWORD

At a moment when the tragic American involvement in Southeast Asia has finally come to a painful end nothing could be more constructive than a hard look at the often hypocritical, sometimes quixotic, and only occasionally logical relationship of the United States and the Philippines.

In a sense the Philippines was where it all began—the flawed, distorted, and confused American adventure on the far side of the Pacific.

To be sure Manila Bay had been preceded by Commander Perry in Japan and Secretary of State Hay's promulgation of the "Open Door" policy toward China. Regardless of the oratorical flourishes which surrounded these two acts they were both, in retrospect, hard-headed Yankee efforts to insure the United States its share of the spoils of trade with the Orient. Yet, not until Admiral Dewey spoke his order: "You may fire when ready, Mr. Gridley," did Theodore Roosevelt's chauvinist "Manifest Destiny" become transformed from rhetoric to reality.

It is both instructive and depressing to note that the rationalization which underpinned Manifest Destiny was just as ramshackle as the justifications invented in our time for the Vietnam intervention.

Americans, generally, find it difficult to keep their attention fixed on the Philippines for any extended period of time, and this has been true from the beginning. Few Americans had ever heard of the islands before the Spanish-American war. Suffused with goodwill and self-congratulation over the liberation of Cuba from Spanish tyranny, and with patriotic pride aroused by Dewey's exploits and his thumbing the nose at the Kaiser, few Americans could understand why the "bandit," Aguinaldo, did not appreciate America's generosity and insisted on fighting a long, bitter guerrilla war (a model of that later led by Ho Chi Minh) against those who had freed the Philippines from Spanish rule.

Nor, alas, were Americans in general much more anxious to hear and to remember the terrible atrocities which their troops committed in the course of the struggle against Aguinaldo (the water-cure and other horrors) than were many Americans who more recently heard of what had happened at My Lai.

Aguinaldo was hardly the first to wage a war of liberation—the Americans themselves had gotten their start with a war of liberation against the English. But he was the first to wage one against the American power, if we except the doomed resistance of the American Indians against superior U.S. firepower.

The history of the U.S.-Philippines relation is more than usually confused. If economic advantage was one string to the American bow and acquisition of an outpost against the fast-expanding Japanese empire another, it was also true that the Americans brought to the islands positive gains—education, public health, technology, and an expanding sense of American democratic institutions and ideals (despite the way we turned these ideals inside-out after 1898).

And, of course, there is the paradox that the United States, after all, did restore independence to the Philippines in the 1930s in what was hailed at the time as an unprecedented gesture of magnanimity. Not so often mentioned is the fact that the trigger for this gesture was economic benefit to American agriculture. Independence ended the serious and costly direct competition of Philippines products, particularly vegetable fats, in the U.S. marketplace.

And formal independence did not sever the American connection. In a sense it made relations closer, warmer. So did the joint war in the Pacific, MacArthur, Back-to-Bataan.

In the post-war era the closeness continued, fueled in part by the Cold War, by a mutual Philippines-American interest in combatting communism. The U.S. had continued to keep its important Philippine bases, and collaboration grew stronger as the Vietnam involvement took shape and gradually turned into the obsession of American policy makers.

The Philippines was proud to number itself among the few Asian democracies. It had taken the U.S. example as model and the United States, too, was proud of this stepchild, proud to point to the Philippines as an argument against colonialism, an argument that democracy not tyranny could be and was viable in Asia.

Nor was this mere propaganda. Ho Chi Minh was so impressed by U.S. policy vis-à-vis the Philippines that in 1945 he proposed to President Truman a similar relationship for Vietnam and the U.S.A. Unfortunately, with Roosevelt dead and the State Department in the control of its Europeanists who strongly supported the French, Ho Chi Minh's valuable proposal was tossed into a pigeonhole and never even answered.

Thus, the United States—which might have made a post-war start in Southeast Asia by taking a radical Nationalist Communist movement under wing and moving into peacetime with a brave new experiment in the spirit of its most successful Asian venture—turned its back and by that act set the stage for the grim tragedy which followed.

And more. In the early post-World War II years the United States tried out in the Phippines many of the anti-guerrilla tactics later so unsuccessfully applied in Vietnam. In the Philippines the tactics had some success. But the American specialists did not get it through their heads that the reason for their success was not the often childish devices which they used but the political dynamism of Magsaysay, who understood that it was not enough to use force to crush communist peasant guerrillas. There must be effective social-economic-political policy as well. This policy must be directed at genuine reform and relief of the critical problems of the peasantry. Otherwise the countryside would continue to afford a safe environment in which communism could grow and prosper. Force was not enough. Genuine social progress was the key.

When the same Americans went to Vietnam they brought with them their bag of Philippines tricks. Some worked in Vietnam. Some did not. But no genuine change was possible in the countryside because the dynamic ingredient—Magsaysay's political program —was absent.

If the story ended here it would be easier to see the lessons. But it does not. Magsaysay's untimely death opened the way to an innovative, charismatic, and power-hungry leader, Marcos. Marcos posed as a democrat but at his first chance he subverted the Philippines' democratic tradition, suspended civil liberties, instituted a rule of force and extinguished the sole American implant of democratic government in Asia.

Moreover, Marcos accomplished this act without stimulating even the faintest whisper of protest from Washington—far too busy supporting other corrupt and dictatorial regimes in Asia to care what had happened to the best and brightest example of U.S. tradition which existed in that hemisphere. Indeed, there was a sigh of relief among some policy architects at the White House, the Pentagon, and the C.I.A.—at least now we have a *reliable* dictator in Manila. No more problems.

But here is where the Philippines story is so instructive. Marcos is not and never was reliable in the sense of Washington's definition. That is, no more than Diem or Thieu or Park was he prepared to put American interests ahead of his own dynastic ambitions. Shrewd and ambitious he could read the political signs as well as anyone. Long before the end in Vietnam he had begun to shift his ground, preparing for pragmatic approaches to the East.

And so the question comes full circle. Who would have been a more staunch ally of America in Asia—a dictator like Marcos or one of his constitutional opponents, a man of principle, a man honest enough to speak back to the U.S. but brave enough to speak up for civil liberties and the democratic process? Who would have been a better friend—a Philippines leader who told Washington frankly that it was wrong in Vietnam or an autocrat who manipulated his views in order to extract the greatest personal advantage? Who would have been the best supporter of the U.S.A. in Asia—a Philippines leader who sought true collaboration with the U.S.A. in an effort to resolve deep social ills or a man who played hard-to-get in order to obtain the arms needed to crush his own people?

If anyone can doubt the answers to these questions, Raul Manglapus has them first hand. He speaks as a constitutionalist, a devout believer in democracy, a former Foreign Minister of his country, a one-time Presidential candidate, a warm and true friend of the United States, a Philippines patriot, and an exile from Marcos' terror-haunted regime. We as well as his countrymen have much to learn from Raul Manglapus.

HARRISON E. SALISBURY

ACKNOWLEDGMENTS

O f the many who have helped me and my family in our trying days of exile I must cite with warmest appreciation William P. Bundy for assistance "beyond the call of friendship." I struck up a warm friendship with Bill during his days as Assistant Secretary of State for Far East Affairs when he cheerfully agreed to change his regional designation to "East Asia and the Pacific" after I had the temerity to question, in a speech before the World Affairs Council of Northern California, the relevance of the term "Far East" to the realities of the post-colonial world. It was Bill who was mainly responsible for, among many other things, helping me obtain a position at Cornell University, where I was provided with unequalled facilities for research on the beginnings of American intervention in my country.

I should next mention, with gratitude and admiration, the Ford Foundation, which—in the face of blandishments from the Marcos dictatorship—lived up to its best traditions and stood firm on its decision to give me a grant for a year of research at Cornell.

I am indebted to Frank Golay who, as head of the Southeast Asia Program, welcomed me to Cornell when he himself was about to leave for a year of teaching at the University of the Philippines. I may have taken unfair advantage of his preparations for departure when I obtained his *nihil obstat*, before he could think twice, to putting down my research in the form of a musical play. The play, *Manifest Destiny*, constitutes the second part of this book.

I am grateful to John Echols, whose light and scholarly hand as acting chairman of the Southeast Asia Program during most of my stay at Cornell was so conducive to relaxed research; Cesar Majul, then visiting professor from the University of the Philippines; John Wolf, professor of linguistics and his wife, Ida; Helen Swank, the incredibly efficient (and charming) administrative officer of the Program—for their valuable suggestions on the play; to Martin Hatch and Don Croker of the Cornell Graduate School of Music for putting down my music on paper with such understanding and love; the generous group of members of the faculty and graduate students who put on a reading and singing of the play for the benefit of the distinguished journalist Tom Buckley and his wife Barbara; and to Tom Buckley for writing the play up so eruditely and sympathetically in the *New York Times*.

At Cornell I relied heavily on George McT. Kahin, professor of government, for advice on moves for the restoration of freedom to my country and for the ideas which I attempt to develop in the chapters that form the first part of this book. Oey Jok Po, of the Cornell Library, was most helpful in introducing me to time-saving techniques in library research.

Thousands of Filipino and American friends have helped to provide forums to which I have been invited to speak on the silencing of Philippine democracy and to suggest steps proposed in the first part of this book that both Filipinos and Americans might take in the reshaping of U. S. policy so that the Filipino will might be less blunted. To them I give my thanks and with them I share a prayer for the early redemption of our democracy.

INTRODUCTION

The ruins of U.S. intervention in Indochina are still burning hot, but the debate has already begun: Resolved, that Thieu and Lon Nol fell because they were abandoned by the United States. In this form, the proposition puts on the affirmative side the domino watchers and those who sincerely lament that the sacrifice of thousands of American lives was made meaningless by the American withdrawal.

The dominoes, it will be argued, have begun to fall. American prestige and credibility have collapsed and Southeast Asian nations have begun to question America's most solemn pledges, even those ratified by the Senate and people of the United States. The first Southeast Asian to ask for a review of military agreements with the United States was Ferdinand Marcos of the Philippines.

Mrs. Marcos, whose lavish world travels with the second string jet set have earned her in the serious U.S. press some informal awards for conspicuous consumption, was recently credited in the *New York Times* with the uncanny ability "to be at the right time and at the right place" when photographers are in sight. Mr. Marcos now displays a parallel ability in the struggle for political survival.

Marcos is now indeed at the right time and at the right place. He is the first of Asian dictators to play on the fears

1

of the American public in the wake of the Indochina debacle. He needs America's support for his dictatorship, and he has seen the growing antipathy in the U.S. Congress towards dictators. He has opened the Philippines to unlimited foreign investment and there, of course, is his ace. If the American people reject him, the American investors may not. Indeed, his successful propaganda thus far has claimed that all American investment would have been thrown out of the country had he not instituted his dictatorship.

The fears of American investors may prevail and Marcos may win his clever, if unoriginal, bluff. America will then continue to supply him with the weaponry with which to repress the forty-four million Filipinos. The domino watchers will be temporarily put at ease until the reality again overcomes the illusion.

The proposition as worded—that Indochina has fallen to the communists because it was abandoned by the United States—is shrouded in the illusion which originated in the 1950s and which many of us in Southeast Asia were persuaded to believe, namely, that communism could be stopped in any given country by supporting a government, *any* government, that declared itself anti-communist, regardless of its relationship with its people.

In 1954, I sat at the Manila Conference as its Secretary-General and I was witness to the institutionalization of this illusion. Eight nations, only three of them Asian, met to draft and sign the treaty that brought SEATO to life.

President Magsaysay gave me the assignment of defending the treaty against its critics. In our flowering democratic system at the time it was a lively debate indeed. The extreme left, of course, would have nothing to do with anything that had to do with the United States. The non-communist, nationalist position, voiced by the late Senator Recto, was that we had demeaned our sovereignty for what, after all, was not even a solid guarantee of our security, since the treaty did not contain the automatic retaliation that is at the heart of the NATO agreement.

The shedding of American blood for Vietnam has since blunted the edge of that argument. But all sides appear now to have missed the essential contradiction in the spirit and letter of the treaty.

The rhetoric of the day had justified it as the alliance of Asian with Western nations to defend democracy. Yet, of the Asian members only one, the Philippines, was a fully operative democracy. Pakistan was still operating under an interim constitution and Thailand was in one of its spells of military rule.

Thailand has just returned to democracy not by SEATO or American intervention but by the shedding of Thai blood in the streets of Bangkok. I was told by Thais of several persuasions and ages in Bangkok in February 1975 that if the army were tempted to take over again the soldiers "would have to kill many more people."

A determined, democratic Thailand, in spite of initial difficulties, is displaying a stability that should disqualify it from the list of unsteady dominoes. Elsewhere in South and Southeast Asian the working democracies like Malaysia and Ceylon cause no worry at all among the domino watchers. They may require grain and economic aid but for them there is no need to alert the U.S. Marines.

A policy of containment by military alliance which disregards the extent of the popular base of the member governments cannot succeed. By now the United States must be convinced that it is the stability that comes with popular government that stops communism and saves American blood and money. Right-wing dictatorships are brittle and will collapse before the advance of an organized ideological force. If the dictatorship lasts long enough, as in Portugal, it drives large numbers of the people to the other extreme. When at last the dictatorship collapses, a return to democracy becomes difficult since it is the Communist party that emerges as the best organized political movement, even though it may command the outright allegiance of a small minority.

So then it seems that the propostion must be reworded: Resolved, that Thieu and Lon Nol fell because they were abandoned by their own people. It is a bitter piece of reality but it should be more comforting to Americans than the half-truth that Thieu and Lon Nol fell due only to the lack of American military support.

The Marcos demand for a revision of Philippine-U.S. military agreements at this time betrays his fear that the bitter reality may overcome the illusion and the American people may at last reject further support for dictators. His demand is calculated to perpetuate the illusion that it is American military support that stops communism and to distract attention from the repression in the Philippines which is in fact, as in Portugal, weakening the fiber of popular resistance to the blandishments of the extreme left.

With U.S. aid and the resources of the Philippine government at his command, Marcos has launched effective overseas propaganda to dress up his repression. Like Park in South Korea, he attempts to persuade the world that the people have accepted his dictatorship by holding occasional referendums that predictably, under conditions of martial law, return overwhelming endorsements of his regime. In other words, Marcos, so the propaganda goes, will not fall because he is supported by the people. Marcos is anti-communist. He has told American investors to "write your own ticket." Therefore, he deserves continued U.S. military support.

With the legislature abolished, the opposition silenced, the press fully controlled, the judiciary subject to summary dismissal, and U.S. policy apparently in acquiescence, an initial atmosphere of resignation and "adjustment to reality" set in among the Filipino people. It was only a surface calm, but Marcos was quick to point to it as evidence that his referendum results were genuine. For a while, it looked as if he was on his way to the successful construction of a "New Society" based on fear and accommodation.

But the Marcos grand design had failed to reckon with the capacity of one institution not only to survive repression but also to resist it—the Church. His technocrats and army advisers, preoccupied with their ivory tower economics and their military tactics, had discounted the growing activism within the Church and preferred wishfully to remember only its past reactionary role, its worldly friars of the nineteenth century, its subsequent embrace of the establishment to hurdle the wall of separation of Church and State introduced by the American occupation.

They underestimated the new social commitment of the priests, nuns, and laymen who are determined to take seriously the call to justice and freedom of the Johannine Revolution. By arresting some of these Church leaders immediately after the declaration of martial law, they expected the institutional Church, i.e., the hierarchy, to order a moral ceasefire, recall the clergy to their convents, and allow the government to, as one enthusiastic technocrat put it, "get things done at last."

Indeed, in the first year and a half of martial law, it seemed as if the Church leaders would repudiate its front liners and retreat to a passive position as the rape of human rights was paraded openly before them. But by the middle of 1974 all eighty-one Roman Catholic bishops had arrived at a consensus. Martial law with its "climate of fear" had to go, and they said so in a formal letter to Marcos.

Meanwhile, the heads of the major religious orders

had organized themselves into an association and become the center of information, counsel, and moral support for the resistance to the dictatorship. They began to publish mimeographed weekly documented reports which gained wide distribution in and out of the country. A year after the declaration of martial law, they released a formal survey which showed that 75 percent of the people thought that the political situation had deteriorated, that crime and corruption had increased, and that the referendums of January and July 1973 were in fact a mockery of the popular will.

In February 1975, this last finding was confirmed by Primitivo Mijares, former President of the National Press Club and head of the Media Advisory Council, which had been placed in charge of press censorship by Marcos. Mijares defected in San Francisco, after having accompanied Mrs. Marcos on her visit to New York, and revealed how he had participated in concocting the results of the two plebiscites in order to give Marcos an "overwhelming" victory.

Mijares' defection came just as Marcos was about to hold another referendum to "renew his popular mandate," his way of temporizing in the face of the growing opposition from the Church. This opposition had just inspired a hunger strike by Eugenio Lopez, Jr., the publisher of the *Manila Chronicle*, who had been under detention for two years. Lopez was joined in his fast by Sergio Osmeña III, grandson of the late President Sergio Osmeña, who returned with General MacArthur to Leyte in 1944, and son of Senator Sergio Osmeña, Jr., who had been Marcos' opponent in the 1969 presidential elections. Lopez and Osmeña were deceived into giving up their fast by promises made by the Defense Secretary Juan Ponce Enrile, which were subsequently repudiated by Marcos. In the U.S., the *New York Times* and *Parade* magazine published articles exposing the manner in which the Lopez detention has been used by Marcos for massive extortion from the wealthy Lopez family.

The February 1975 referendum produced the same predictable near-unanimous popular endorsement of Marcos, and immediately successive weekly reports of the Association of Major Religious Superiors came out with documentation condemning the new farce. Their March 7, 1975, report, chastising those who would not speak up against the mockery, quoted Peter Weiss: "You could see it and while you looked on it and did not revolt against it, you consented to it."

Most prominent among the many who do not consent is Benigno Aquino, Jr., the Senator who might have been the opposition candidate for president in 1973 had not the Marcos *coup* cancelled the elections. At this writing Aquino is near death in a fast protesting the dictatorship. Marcos appears unmoved. Aquino has been his unforgiveable tormentor, the impish, relentless articulator of popular resentment against the excesses of the Marcos family. Aquino was credited with almost all important exposés, most devastating of which was that which unmasked Marcos' deceitful handling of the Muslims which eventually led to their rebellion.

"Take out Marcos and martial law and there will be peace," a Filipino Muslim told *New York Times* correspondent Joseph Lelyveld in March 1975. "We can coexist as we have coexisted for the last 400 years with our Christian brothers." Our proud Muslim brothers can not forget the terrorism with which the Marcos machine defeated the Muslim leaders who had been in opposition to him in the last three elections before martial law.

Most of all the Muslims cannot forget the *Jabidah* massacre. Marcos—when already seated as president and ignoring the obvious ethical questions raised by his move—obtained the power-of-attorney of a section of the heirs of the Sultan of Sulu to pursue the claim to Sabah (then already part of Malaysia), which included not only the demand for sovereignty but also a substantial money claim. As the ranking member of our party in the Philippine Senate Foreign Relations Committee, I had opposed the claim in the context of our regional relations at the time.

To provide tactical backing for his Sabah plans, Marcos conceived a project, codenamed *Jabidah,* which recruited Filipino Muslims to be trained secretly on Corregidor Island off Manila Bay for the infiltration of Sabah. When told of their mission to fight fellow Muslims in a neighboring land, the trainees balked and demanded to be returned home. They were then loaded into trucks, driven to the airfield on the pretext that they were to be flown home and then massacred. All, including a Christian army officer who had objected to the massacre, died, except one trainee, Jibin Arula, who, though severely wounded, managed to swim ashore in Cavite province and tell all. The press exposed the plot and the massacre and Aquino delivered a privileged speech which sparked a Senate investigation. The Malaysians withdrew their ambassador from Manila.

In predictable reaction to Marcos' change of the ground rules, the Muslim Independence Movement was born in 1968, with full independence as a maximum objective but, many felt, with substantial autonomy within the framework of the Philippine Republic as a possible compromise. They were to pursue their ends mainly by peaceful means—not by open rebellion.

In 1972, as co-leader of the progressives in the Constitutional Convention, I had agreed with Muslim delegates—notably Domocao Alonto of the older generation and Michael Mastura of the younger—to sign a declaration calling on the Convention to grant certain

Muslim-dominated areas in Mindanao and Sulu the fullest autonomy possible under the forthcoming new constitution and within the sovereign scope of the Philippine Republic.

Before we could act on the amendment, Marcos declared martial law, allowing the Convention to continue to sit so that he might ram through it a "transitory provision" making him permanent dictator. At the same time, as correspondent Lelyveld reports, "martial law foreclosed the Muslim claim to local power." The Muslims were ordered to surrender their defensive household firearms which, reacting the way most Americans under similar conditions would react, they refused to do. The movement then broke into open rebellion. Marcos' adventurism provoked open intervention from Muslim nations in West Asia and Africa.

Negotiations in Jeddah between Marcos' envoys and representatives of the rebels collapsed in 1974. It is not difficult to understand why. On the one hand the Muslims harbor a bitter hurt and a deep mistrust of Marcos and on the other Marcos has no use for a final settlement since this would mean one less excuse for continuing martial law and soliciting U.S. military support.

And so Marcos plays the game of many contradictions. He lobbies for U. S. aid while he threatens to review the U. S. military position in the Philippines. He swears into his government Soviet-oriented Marxists while he cries "Communist!" He sends his wife to embrace Mao Tse-Tung while he fights the Maoists. He drops Israel for Muslim oil while he kills Muslims in Sulu. All this would add up to admirable *Realpolitik* were it not a brazen effort to make his dictatorship viable and justify the killing of Philippine democracy.

This book will show how, like American democracy, Philippine democracy as of 1972 was imperfect. It will also show that, like the imperfect American Republic in its bicentennial year, the Philippine Republic in its twenty-sixth year was not yet ready for the executioner's block. For like the American Republic, the Philippine Republic possessed within itself the capacity to straighten itself out.

The last word in this introduction is addressed to my American friends through whom I, as an exile, should express my appreciation for freedom in America. I first learned about freedom in America from my American Jesuit teachers in Manila. I experience it now as it affords me the uncensored facilities of the published word to circulate my thoughts, even those that challenge American policy in my country.

I must share also with my American friends what many of them must now be lamenting—the realization that in the fight for freedom in the Philippines today neither Jefferson nor Lincoln is any longer being invoked. In the far South it is the Koran, in some hills it is Mao Tse-Tung, and among the majority in the plains and cities it is the Christian theology of liberation.

Something has gone wrong with America in the Philippines. The taste of Bataan has turned sour. America no longer speaks the language of freedom but of profits, not of democacy but of "stability." Where did it all go wrong? Perhaps, to suggest a clue, in the beginning?

To uncover this clue I have included in this book the musical play which I had the temerity to write at Cornell in my first year of exile. It is not entirely fair, perhaps, to judge Teddy Roosevelt and his Manifest Destiny in post-Indochina terms. But to understand America in Southeast Asia and the Philippines today, it is necessary to go back to that winter afternoon in Washington, D. C., when, as Assistant Secretary of the Navy, he took advantage of the absence of the Secretary to order Dewey to sink the Spanish Fleet in Manila Bay.

For in these days of remorse and reconciliation, there is some peril in heeding the call to forget the destructive past and think only of the constructive future. I prefer to heed the tested injunction that one who forgets the past is condemned to repeat it.

RAUL S. MANGLAPUS

MARTIAL LAW:
INTRODUCTION TO DICTATORSHIP

On September 21, 1972, I left Manila for two weeks of speaking engagements in California. Martial law was declared the day after.

It was so narrow an escape that the question of whether or not I had advance notice of the declaration is still debated in circles interested in Philippine affairs. Those who are avid for the Ian Fleming brand of international intrigue seem to favor the fascinating explanation that I was told to leave by an American intelligence agency in order to be some kind of reserve American boy in case the Marcos-centered plan (presumably conceived by the same agency) should collapse.

When this rumor reached my ears, I was hard put not to act in any way that might appear to confirm it. For instance, when I later accepted an invitation to Windsor by the Canadian Institute of International Affairs, I was careful to spell out to some of my associates at Cornell that I was being sent a round-trip ticket by the C.I.I.A. and not by any other organization *idem sonans!*

Upon landing in Honolulu, I decided—in view of the uncertainty of the situation—to cancel my speaking engagements and remain only a few days to work on stabilizing my stay in the United States and to find ways of getting my family to join me. I had had my share of prison—two years with the Japanese Kempeitai—and I was not about to go flying home to the brand new stockades set up by Marcos.

It was in Honolulu that I read the first press reports about the series of arrests and the edicts issued in that initial week of martial law. And it was in Honolulu that I read the most biting press opinion against Marcos' action that I have yet encountered anywhere in the United States.

This may have been due to Hawaii's geographical proximity to the Philippines, or to the fact of its substantial Filipino population. But there may have been a deeper reason. Could there be in the Hawaiian subconscious a violent revulsion to the slightest hint of martial law? For it was in Hawaii that there occurred the most recent and perhaps the only state-wide American experience of this emergency condition.

Some Hawaiians can still recall that experience. Some to this day cannot accept the constitutionality of what transpired, believing that the military alone, in the words of Jim Richstad of the East-West Center, "cannot under the guise of martial law subvert civil government or the constitutional guarantees of American citizens who are neither in disorder or subversive."

The United States Supreme Court appears to have approximated this view. In the case of *Duncan v. Kahanamoku* (327 U.S. 304) the Court voided military trials of citizens under the Hawaiian Organic Act—which did not intend to permit a form of martial law that would be contrary to American political philosophy and institutions.

Justice Douglas, speaking with the majority, warned that the Hawaiian experience, however well intentioned, "is a precedent to avoid . . . even in the darkest hour."

December 1941, was indeed a dark hour in Hawaii. There was a real war upon it, not an artificial emergency concocted by covetous politicians. Pearl Harbor had been bombed, there were fears of outright invasion, and the multi-racial complex of its society offered no special assurance of solidarity in the face of the crisis.

Great lamentation has been heard over the alleged excesses of *that* martial law government: yet compared to the most recent version of the same formula across the Pacific, an account of the Hawaiian experience reads like a tourist brochure depicting a care-free and unfettered island community.

True, Hawaiian martial law had its absurd moments— when even cookbooks had to be submitted to censorship. However, no Honolulu newspaper or radio was permanently shut down. There was licensing and censorship on war news; but no newspaper publisher or editor was imprisoned, nor was any opposition politician, dissenting intellectual, or progressive priest.

The Hawaiian experience is relevant, because the Philippine constitutional law relies heavily on American jurisprudence.

We have been told, however, that it is not the 1941 Hawaiian model but the 1862 proclamation of Abraham Lincoln that is the historical precedent for the September 1972 decision in Manila. The Lincoln proclamation was issued on September 24, 1862, and it was, in its wording and implementation, remarkably selective.

To begin with, a real civil war was in progress. Lincoln specifically subjected rebels, insurgents, and their aiders and abettors to martial law. He suspended the writ of habeas corpus and instituted trial and punishment of rebels by military courts. However, history records no case of newspapers being shut down or of publishers, priests, and industrialists being arrested by Lincoln's soldiers. Under the guise of martial law, did Lincoln ever arrest a society columnist for making his First Lady uncomfortable with her "light comment?" Marcos did.

On the other hand, did Marcos secure from Congress,

as Lincoln did, statutory confirmation of his resolution? No. Marcos abolished Congress.

The extent of valid implementation of Lincoln's proclamation was in fact tested in the U.S. Supreme Court case *Ex Parte Milligan* (4 Wall 2, 1866), which holds that military commissions established in a state not invaded or engaged in rebellion had no jurisdiction to try an ordinary citizen.

Justice Davis, delivering the majority opinion, ruled that martial law which suspends all civil rights and their remedies and subjects citizens as well as soldiers to the absolute will of the commander "destroys every constitutional guarantee" and that "civil liberty and this kind of martial law cannot endure together; the antagonism is irreconcilable; and, in the conflict, one or the other must perish."

The court then went on to provide posterity with the ultimate test for the validity of martial law. Martial law, it said, cannot be applied "where the courts are open and in their process unobstructed."

In September 1972 the Philippine courts were open and unobstructed. They are even more open and unobstructed today, for Marcos proudly boasts of complete law and order. Where, then, is the constitutional justification for martial law?

The Lincolnian model turned out to be for Marcos not a model at all, but a contradiction to his claims of American jurisprudential support for his plot against Philippine democracy.

The defenders of Marcos, invoking precedents on martial law, are in fact evading the central constitutional issue. Even Marcos has stopped pretending that he is running the Philippines under the martial law provisions of the 1934 constitution. He has proclaimed a new constitution which gives him dictatorial powers and places in his hands the authority to decide when those powers shall be delivered to an elected parliament and prime minister.

Marcos secured this new constitution by manipulating the Constitutional Convention which was in session in September 1972 and which is never mentioned by his propagandists abroad, for that story betrays the heart of the conspiracy.

The Constitutional Convention was pressed upon Congress and the president by the Filipino people themselves, to solve the problems of the country which demanded far-ranging, peaceful, and fundamental structural change and the free choice of ideological alternatives. Nobody called these problems trifling; yet they were not peculiarly Filipino problems nor were they ever grounds for dictatorial action. General Romulo described the Filipino situation at that time when he spoke before the Commonwealth Club of California in May 1973 as "the darker depths of democracy—the bickering, the factionalism, the corruption, the aimless drift, the rebellion of the alienated." He referred to "the smoke screen of self-interests, the distortion of privilege." (When I showed these passages to an American friend, he thought Romulo was describing Washington, D.C., in 1975!)

The Rand Corporation, the prestigious American research firm, was commissioned by the U.S. Agency for International Development to do a study on Philippine conditions. Hardly a year before martial law, a report was filed with such conclusions as these:

1. "The political system appears to be stable and generally responsive to the desire of most people."

2. "The economy appears to be performing better than commonly thought and is spread broadly across the country."

3. "Crime is not a national problem. Violence and fear of violence are concentrated in a few areas."

4. "The HMB (the dissident group) are not a serious threat to the government. The success of the HMB rests in a large measure on what they do rather than on the conditions of the Philippine society."

Marcos, in his book *Today's Revolution: Democracy,* published a few months before September 1972, etched a picture of Philippine conditions even rosier than the Rand Corporation dared to report. Both Marcos and the Rand Corporation agreed that democracy in the Philippines was working, that Filipinos had serious problems, but these could be solved within the democratic system.

This, also, is how the Filipino people felt. They rallied massively to force Congress to implement a democratic solution: to call a Constitutional Convention, free of the artificial advantage enjoyed by the two major parties, free of incumbent Senators and Congressmen, free to chart a new course for the Republic.

The Constitutional Convention was not convoked in response to any constitutional requirement for periodic revision of the fundamental charter. There was no such requirement. It was the people, speaking through massive demonstrations supported by a wide spectrum of forces ranging from farmers' movements and student activists to religious confraternities and Rotarians, who prevailed on a reluctant Congress to call it and to change the electoral rules so that independent candidates might have a fair chance at being elected delegates.

In the Convention elections, it was my good fortune to be elected as one of eighteen delegates for the largest constituency in the country, the first district of the province of Rizal. Of the 320 delegates, there were enough progressives and independents to make a strong force. Although it was not strong enough to elect the convention president, it was of sufficient numbers to control, under the Convention rules, some of the important committees.

I was chosen Chairman of the Committee on Suffrage and Electoral Reforms. All but one of the reforms that our Committee reported out were passed by the convention. The voting age was lowered to eighteen, voting was made compulsory, and constitutional protection was given to all political parties. Only the proposal to allow Filipinos abroad to vote was lost by a small margin of votes. Many of the delegates simply could not see how this could be done efficiently and without fraud.

It was a surprise to us that Mr. Marcos did not move to stop the key electoral reform that would revolutionize the party system and allow the peaceful rise of new ideological forces that might later prove to be his antagonists. We wondered whether he had finally decided to yield to the will of the people. We were to learn later, a little too late, that he had other plans for using the Convention.

PROSTITUTION
OF THE CONVENTION

The Convention opened in June 1971, and by June 1972 there was no longer any doubt that President Marcos controlled it. Eduardo Quintero, a 72-year-old delegate from the province of Leyte and a former ambassador—so honest and so eager that in his waning years he would not be a party to fraud against the people—stood on the floor of the Convention to denounce the distribution of money in envelopes to a number of delegates. He had traced the envelopes to the Presidential Palace. The next day, while he lay in a hospital suffering from high blood pressure, the Palace rewarded him with a full-dress raid on his house by agents of the National Bureau of Investigation who "found" 300,000 pesos in an unlocked drawer. Quintero, the accuser, found himself accused of having received the money from the opposition in order to smear the first family. (In the ensuing investigation a young assistant to the President signed an affidavit attesting to these attempts of the first family to corrupt the delegates. When martial law was declared this man was forced into hiding, but later escaped. He is now in the United States.)

The first evident objective of President Marcos was to get the Convention delegates to change the presidential system to the parliamentary system so that he might continue in power as Prime Minister, since he could no longer run for president. The second was to defeat a resolution filed by members of our group that would ban past and incumbent presidents and their spouses from running for any office under the new constitution.

By the middle of September 1972, he had already achieved both objectives. But in the meantime a kind of crisis had begun to irk the population of the Manila area. It was a sort of ready-made, instant "mess." Bombs were being exploded in the oddest places. Only one person was killed—a shopper in a department store. Most of the bombs were placed in toilets, including the lavatory of the Constitutional Convention. This led an irrepressible retired jurist to remark in a speech on Law Day that he could not accept the official explanation that this was all part of a communist conspiracy, since he could not believe that communists could really be plotting a revolution by constipation!

It was in this tragicomic atmosphere that I left Manila. That morning I had consulted with leaders of my Convention group. It was our opinion that President Marcos, having achieved all that we thought he had wanted from the Convention, would not take any drastic steps until perhaps later should he find that he could not continue in power in spite of the advantages he had gained.

We miscalculated his intentions. He declared martial law on September 22. The immediate cause, officially announced, was an attempt on the life of the Secretary of National Defense. However, a report to the Committee on Foreign Relations of the United States Senate by two staff members sent to Manila in November 1972 stated: "The fact of the matter is that the attempt against the Secretary of Defense occurred on the evening of September 22, the day before the declaration of martial law was announced but, as it turned out, the day after the declaration had been signed."

At 1:30 in the morning on September 23, soldiers were sent to my house to arrest me. They did not believe my wife when she told them I was abroad. They searched the entire house. Simultaneously, two members of the Senate were being successfully apprehended, Senators Jose W. Diokno and Benigno Aquino, Jr. In quick succession others were arrested, including another Senator, Ramon Mitra; the publisher of the *Manila Times*, Joaquin P. Roces; the publisher of the *Philippines Free Press*, Teodora Locsin; former Senator Francisco Rodrigo; and other newspaper editors and writers. In the days following, priests, student leaders, and scores of Constitutional Convention delegates, including my co-leader of the progressive bloc, Teopisto Guingona, Jr., were taken to the stockade.

At first it seemed strange that after arresting so many delegates President Marcos should allow the Convention to continue its sessions. In early October his reason became evident. The opposition had underestimated the President's capacity for detailed planning. He was going to use the Convention to legitimize his power grab and constitutionalize his future dictatorship. Rammed through the Convention was a transitory provision for an interim national assembly composed of the members of Congress and the Convention delegates who had voted for the proposal. It also made President Marcos, in effect, an interim dictator.

This was the heart of the conspiracy. The provision ratified all the acts of the present President under martial law regardless of whether these acts were legitimately within his rights under the 1935 Constitution. It vested all power of government in him and left it to him to decide when to call the interim national assembly to session. Since it was this assembly that was empowered to call the first regular elections under the new constitution,

President Marcos could simply desist from convening it and stay in absolute power indefinitely.

The whole new constitution had to be ratified by the people. To forestall the reopening of Congress under the old constitution, set for every fourth Monday of January, President Marcos called a formal plebiscite on January 15. The call itself was illicit since only the Congress or, as some commentators would claim, the Convention itself could fix the time for a plebiscite.

Thus the people were given only a few weeks to study the new constitution before approving it. A period of free discussion was proclaimed, during which opponents of the new charter were allowed to use radio, television, and a limited space in the controlled press. When it became evident that opposition to the new constitution was so strong that no amount of manipulation could possibly bring about a "yes" vote, President Marcos suddenly announced the postponement of the plebiscite "until February or March." He stopped the right of free discussion, charging his opponents with making use of the "privilege" in order to circulate subversive ideas.

However, merely postponing the plebiscite did not solve his predicament. The Congress could then convene on January 22. Word reached President Marcos that the Senators were planning to subpoena their colleagues held under detention, order their release, and in other ways confront the President with a Senate opposed to martial law. Marcos then took the step that might yet be his undoing. He announced the convening of "citizens assemblies" to be consulted on various matters, including their views on martial law, the reopening of Congress, and the new constitution.

The hastily marshaled assemblies were of course convened *before* January 22 and it was before that date that the historic farce was enacted. President Marcos went on television and radio and revealed that the citizens assemblies had been ratifying bodies and that they had *viva voce* approved the new constitution. He was, therefore, proclaiming the constitution as of that moment, but suspending the sections dealing with the interim national assembly, since the citizens assemblies had voiced objections to convene it. (This saved him the trouble of resisting pressure to convene it; one could never tell what an assembly in session might do.)

Marcos now rules as a constitutional authoritarian, a euphemism for a de facto tyrant.

THE AMBIDEXTROUS "REVOLUTION"

The Philippines had been "re-feudalized" by a coalition of development administrators (alias "technocrats"), international civil servants (alias World Bank and International Monetary Fund officials), and militarists. This is the theory of Professor Robert Stauffer of the University of Hawaii, and it is difficult to take issue with it (see "Philippine Martial Law: The Political Economy of Refeudalization," paper presented at the annual meeting of the Association for Asian Studies, Boston, April 1–3, 1974).

But is this coalition using Marcos, or is it vice versa? When martial law was declared in 1972, Marcos was coming to the end of his second and last term as President.

A few questions bear asking:

What if the Philippine Constitution had, as in the pre-Truman U.S. Constitution, imposed no limits to the number of presidential terms for one incumbent? Would Marcos then have found it necessary or desirable at that precise point to declare martial law in order to continue in power? Might Marcos not in fact have chosen to side with the nationalists and, using his awesome presidential powers, get himself elected over and over again?

If his final term had not been ending soon, would

Marcos have felt the urge to publish his ambidextrous vision entitled *Today's Revolution: Democracy?* It is now an open secret that the ghost-writer of that book was a sincere and dedicated Marxist, one of several in the inner circle of Marcos. For all the fighting rhetoric in the name of "human freedom" in the final chapter, the rest of the book is a systematic denigration of Philippine democracy and of the capacity of the Filipino to solve his problems without the sacrifice of individual rights. It even denigrates the 1896 revolutionists whom recent neo-Marxist reappraisal cannot forgive for having allowed themselves to be led by members of the elite.

There is no vision in that book of an authoritarian coalition with the technocrats, militarists, and multinational corporations. However, there is wistful reference to "opposition politicians . . . occasionally sequestered," to militarism as the "instrument of national unification" for the new nations as well as for the "then developing Western countries," and to "restrictions on freedom long customary" among Western nations.

But the ultimate vision in this book is not a dictatorship that is unmistakably of the right. There is no mention of the virtues of foreign investment, no glorification of Gross National Product. On the contrary, after a half-hearted blanket denunciation of totalitarianism, a distinction is made in favor of communist dictatorship since it "justified itself with the socialization of wealth."

Marcos' Marxist ghost-writer must have been delighted that Marcos was willing to affix his name to a tract that prepared the way for authoritarianism, even if that authoritarianism might have provisionally to be of the right. At the very least, the experience would condition the Filipinos to accept government by decree and the elimination of personal liberties. As an incisive Marxist, he must have been confident that the totalitarianism on the right, supervised by the coalition correctly described by Robert Stauffer, would eventually prove itself powerless to solve the overriding problem of wealth and poverty. He must have foreseen, as qualified observers like former American presidential advisor Clayton Fritchley now sees, that Marcos' "New Society" would only make the "superwealthy" wealthier and the poor more destitute.

And he must now foresee that a stubborn U.S. policy will continue to support Marcos for the sake of stability and profits to the point where the silenced democratic forces will be so debilitated that there will be no recourse but to veer all the way to the left. At this point, the traditional anti-communism of U.S. policy will have met another tragic *denouement:* it will not only have helped to destroy a democracy; it will have assisted in the delivery of a new communist state.

But while we might at that point mourn the paradoxical effect of U.S. policy, we may not have to mourn Marcos. He is no army sergeant like Batista, guileless and crude. He is a consummate political gambler and, having failed with his wager on the right, he may not hesitate to take his final chances with a finesse to the left. His vision—created with deliberate ambidexterity by his ghost-writer—certainly allows for such a move. Thus, unlike Cuba, the Philippines will not need to wait for a new leader for a revolution on the left. Ferdinand Marcos will be happy to be his own Fidel Castro. And it may become a little awkward for the U.S. to try to keep Clark Field and Subic Bay as it has Guantanamo.

INSTABILITY AND DECEPTION

Americans are fast coming to recognize the essential instability that Marcos has injected into the political life of the nation. The Valeo Report, read into the U.S. Senate Record by Senator Mansfield in December 1973, warned that the question of legal succession now "threatens to be thrown into complete chaos." Furthermore, the freedom of expression, that safety valve on which the Rand Corporation report relied for its optimism concerning the Filipino picture, is now gone, and pent up bitterness may soon erupt.

A staff report to the Foreign Relations Committee of the U.S. Senate reveals that the official explanation for martial law given the committee staff members in Manila was that Marcos feared "four distinct but allegedly related plots with the common objective of seizing power: a Communist conspiracy, a Muslim independence movement, a Christian Socialist Movement, and a rightist revolution and coup d'état."

The communist movement in the Philippines is nowhere near the peak of its strength as in the days when Ramon Magsaysay dealt with it without suspending civil liberties.

The Muslim Independence Movement has been in existence for several years and was somewhat quiescent until martial law was declared and a showdown was precipitated over the issue of surrender of arms. It is the question of land which is at the root of the Muslim problem. The Muslims look on land ownership through the prism of the Koran, the Sunnah, and other Muslim customary laws. The Torrens system of land ownership, imported from Australia, is effective in Christian areas. It is, however, in irreconcilable conflict with Muslim land tenure traditions.

Some progressive Muslim leaders, including delegates to the Constitutional Convention, were about to issue a joint manifesto with the Christian Social Movement proposing constitutional autonomy for Muslims in selected areas of Mindanao and Sulu, where they might govern themselves under their traditional laws within a quasi-federal framework. A measure of constitutional autonomy would have provided the Muslims with the opportunity to make their own system work for themselves.

This proposal for autonomy was forgotten with martial law. Instead Marcos invited the Muslims into open rebellion with his demand for their surrender of their defensive household weapons.

The Christian Social Movement (CSM) was organized in 1967 to launch a progressive alliance broadly based on the working class. It embraced those in all classes who favored peaceful change, offering what it thought the people really desired—an indigenous political ideology that could reorganize Philippine society and that would harmonize social justice with individual dignity. To men desperate to cling to their power, the CSM might have easily looked like a subversive plot to seize power. To many Filipinos it had become a hopeful alternative for peaceful revolution.

The Philippine Government spokesmen have oscillated so often between blaming the left and the right that

it is difficult to take on face value any grand revelations of
"evidence uncovered." If the crude, amateurish and, as it
turned out, apparently demented assassination attempt
on Mrs. Marcos is the sort of evidence of plots that is
referred to, then the Marcoses can relax, lift martial law,
and launch a campaign for the more intense promotion
of mental health among our harried population.

Accusations of subversion have always been the last
refuge of those with false claims for retention of power.
In 1891, the Philippine national hero, Jose Rizal, in the
foreword to his novel *El filibusterismo,* warned that "the
spectre of subversion has been used so often to frighten
us that, from being a nursery tale, it has acquired a real
and positive existence."

We shall again and again be told of this positive existence. And we shall be told of the positive answer. Not
just armed suppression, but land reform. The whole
country has been declared a land reform area and the
government will make appeals for financial support. Yet
the land reform program (in the launching of which I
had the privilege of participating as the principal spon-
sor of the land reform code in the Senate) is in shambles.
What was to have been an orderly process of redemption
of the landless tenant after the pattern proven successful
in Japan and Taiwan has turned into "instant social justice." This is only a glib slogan which first raised and is
now dashing the hopes of the tenant, since exceptions
have been allowed for retention of the land by the land-
lord which have resulted in thousands of tenants being
evicted from the land instead of becoming its owners.
(These evictions were denounced by the Archbishop of
Manila, Jaime L. Sin, in an international press conference on November 23, 1974.)

Marcos now claims that law and order and content-
ment reign. There is little crime because there is little

crime reported in the controlled press. Nothing is printed about rampant kidnappings, about the robbing of banks. Marcos claims to have abolished private armies, collected a fabulous number of illegal arms, and imprisoned warlords.

A report from Manila published on June 2, 1973, in the *Washington Post* contains a stunning refutation of this claim. A very close associate of President Marcos had been dramatically arrested and imprisoned immediately after declaration of martial law. He had been known to be the warlord with the largest private army and a suspected gun runner. His imprisonment had caused many Filipinos to rejoice and to wonder whether at last Marcos was beginning to mean business. He was later quietly released. The *Washington Post* reported that he openly set up office as the agent for Soviet aircraft and shipping.

In the U.S. we are free to read reliable news about the Philippines because the American press is free. But my poor countrymen at home are not so privileged. They know little of what is going on even in their own communities. President Marcos has gone on television and announced the proclamation of an edict against rumor mongering, an offense so vaguely defined that anyone indulging in a bit of innocent gossip may be taken to the stockades.

In desperation, Manila propagandists are turning to odious comparisons. It is alleged that the strong army rule is needed to develop any country in Asia, and the case of General Suharto and the Indonesian army are triumphantly pointed to as an example. I have met Indonesian friends who resent this comparison. They have reminded me that Suharto and the Indonesian Army, for all their failings, are acting to move Indonesians *toward* democracy, which they never enjoyed under Sukarno. Marcos is doing the opposite. He is moving

Filipinos *away* from democracy, which they have always enjoyed, towards a permanent dictatorship of the worst kind—promoted, not for a recognizable ideology, but for the ambition of one man.

I respect the officers and men of the Philippine armed forces. It is not difficult to see that they, particularly those who were not privy to the plans for the declaration of martial law, had very little choice once it was declared. The Constitution does give the President the power to declare martial law in cases of insurrection, invasion, rebellion, or imminent danger thereof, and it was not their part to determine whether such conditions in fact existed. It was their part to obey their commander-in-chief.

But now these officers and men must be experiencing a traumatic examination of conscience. The proclamation of the new Constitution was patently invalid. The people must certainly think so. And this conviction must have been confirmed by the recent indecisive resolution of the Supreme Court, which after 245 pages of discussion could only conclude that there were not enough votes among the justices to fulfill the legal minimum to declare the proclamation of the new Constitution invalid. The Chief Justice of the Supreme Court, Roberto Concepción, resigned after the resolution was issued and two months before reaching his retirement age, in obvious protest against the proclamation of the new Constitution.

It is the 1934 Constitution, and not the new one, that must be considered in force. But under the 1934 Constitution, Ferdinand E. Marcos was to cease to be President and Commander-in-chief at noon on December 30, 1973. Thereafter it would no longer be the duty of the armed forces to obey him.

Marcos worried about army doubts. He called for a

second showing of his notorious "citizens' assemblies," this time reinforced with a Commission on Elections newly packed with his most faithful henchmen (the former staunchly honest chairman and commissioners had been fired). On July 27, 1973, the question was asked: Do you want President Marcos to continue beyond 1973 and finish the reforms he has initiated under martial law?" The answer, of course, was a resounding, prefabricated "yes." The whole farce merely deepened the cynicism of the people and certainly did not impress the skeptical members of the armed forces who were privy to the process of prefabrication.

PRESIDENTIAL POWER:
A PHILIPPINE LESSON

Under the banners of a third party hastily put together by the political heirs of our late great President Ramon Magsaysay, I once had the temerity to run for president. I stood on a negative issue, the need to destroy the monopoly of the two artificial major parties exclusively protected by law at the counting of the ballots, and also on the positive issue of the decentralization of presidential powers.

When the quixotic battle was over, my supporters consoled themselves with the thought that I had perhaps been saved from an impossible situation. If I had been elected president I would have immediately had to propose constitutional amendments to divest myself of powers—something which many political commentators have seen to be a very difficult thing for a political executive to do. When I was in the Senate, Senator Ferdinand Marcos eloquently supported a decentralization bill which I was sponsoring on the floor. By the time it passed the lower house, Marcos had already been elected president. He, of course, vetoed it.

The passionate advocates of the parliamentary system both in the United States and in the Philippines are enjoying a triumphant moment. Their most dismal predictions have apparently been fulfilled. It is now their boast that had the founding fathers of America opted for the parliamentary system (which after all was their heritage from the English mother country), Americans would not have had to be confronted with the prolonged agonies of Watergate. And the Filipinos, having then adopted the external forms of the same system from America, would now not have to endure Marcos and the criminal destruction of our civil liberties.

It is in fact a paradox of American life that while Americans, perhaps quite unconsciously, accept the parliamentary system in their myriad business corporations, labor unions, and civic associations, they do not seem ready to accept it in their federal and state politics. Alistair Cooke suggests that it was the sheer size of their country that forced the founding fathers to turn away from the English model. At the same time, he adds that, in the search for centralized power, they did toy with an institution the British also possessed—a monarchy. But they did not toy long with it, and finally settled for a compromise. Arthur Schlesinger, Jr., explains that "as victims of what they considered a tyrannical royal prerogative, they were determined to fashion for themselves a Presidency that would be strong but still be limited."

However, Schlesinger also contends, that "strong but limited" president "has now become, with the possible exception of Mao Tse Tung, the most absolute monarch among the great powers of the world."

It is good that Schlesinger chose carefully his words "among the great powers of the world," for there is at least one president who constitutionally is a more absolute monarch than any American President. He is the President of the Republic of the Philippines.

I cannot really say, lest I be challenged on technical grounds, that no president of the United States has ever destroyed *constitutional democracy,* for mention of democracy was carefully avoided in the Convention of 1787.

(Washington seems to have equated it with political parties, which he distrusted without reservation.) I *will* say that no American president has yet succeeded totally in destroying *liberty,* and *that* word is found in the American Declaration of Independence and in the Constitution. And I will also say that a Philippine President has succeeded in destroying liberty *and* democracy—both of which are solemnly enshrined in the Preamble of the Philippine Constitution.

If absolute monarchical power has not enabled an American president to kill human rights, infinite presidential power has permitted a Philippine president to do precisely that.

It all began in 1934, when the delegates to the Constitutional Convention, laying the foundations for independence by leave of the U.S. Tyding-McDuffie Act, agreed that the American separation of powers and presidential system were worthy of emulation indeed—but not the American federal system. There simply was no apparent historical basis to divide the country—already united by race, religion, and revolution—into autonomous states. Therefore, a Presidential Unitary Government was designed, and all the powers of the American presidency and of the American state governors were massed together and deposited in the office of the President of the Philippines.

Furthermore, the convention succumbed to the common historical sin of similar bodies—that of allowing contemporary events to exert a disproportional influence on their deliberations. Impressed by the strong hand of Franklin Delano Roosevelt—and unimpressed by the unspectacular attempts of the Supreme Court to curb him—and swept along by the tide of near-total adulation for Manuel L. Quezon (who was certain to be their first Chief Executive), the delegates invested the

Philippine President with power not only over local governments, but also over Congress.

The Philippine President, for example, was given the item veto over appropriation, revenue, and tariff bills. To over-ride a veto on increases of over ten percent in general appropriations or the public debt, a vote of three-fourths of all the members of each house had to be obtained. In the American Congress, all vetoes require only a two-thirds vote in each house, counted not from all members but only from those present and voting during a quorum.

The *coup de grace,* as it were, was the limitation of Congressional sessions to one-hundred days a year. The President could then call special sessions of at most thirty days each to legislate on subject matter he alone could select. This novel arrangement permitted the Senators and Congressmen a rather generous series of recesses, but it also put them at the mercy of presidential power.

The most spectacular, pregnant, and challenging of the presidential powers are those connected with his office of Commander-in-Chief. It is these that have permitted the Philippine president to surround the demolition of democracy with the claim of constitutionality.

There is nothing scandalous about crowning the head of state in the presidential system with the title of Commander-in-Chief. However, in various instances in Latin American, Indonesian, Korean, U.S., and Philippine constitutions, the obvious justification for it is that in a republican presidential democracy, the military must be the servant and not the master of the people.

The debate begins when the question is asked: "What else comes with the title besides the negative power to insure civilian control of the military?" It is clear in the American and Philippine Constitutions that the president may not, relying on his title as Commander-in-

Chief, unilaterally declare war. Only Congress can do that. But once Congress does so, it is the President's duty—not his right—to conduct the war to a successful conclusion.

This and nothing more would seem to have been the intent of the American and Philippine Constitutional Conventions. As Schlesinger suggests, the President as Commander-in-Chief was to have "no more authority than the First General of the Army, or the First Admiral of the Navy would have had as professional military men." This authority was limited to issuing "orders to the Armed Forces within a framework established by Congress."

Cornell Professor George Kahin has written provocatively on the dramatic and alarming extension of American presidential war-making powers drawn from loose interpretations of the Southeast Asia Treaty Organization (SEATO). I had the privilege of being the Secretary-General at the conference at which SEATO was born, and it is difficult to resist the urge to plunge into the controversy on this aspect of presidential power.

However, this for the moment is not a pressing Philippine Constitutional problem. What now ails the Philippines is not caused by any power of the Philippine president to make war on *other* people. The tragedy is that the delegates to the 1934 Convention, and the electorate by their ratification, are now alleged to have presented to the Philippine president, in the Commander-in-Chief clause, unlimited power to make war on the Filipino people themselves.

In 1941, President Franklin Delano Roosevelt's technique of invoking the Commander-in-Chief clause and presenting Congress with *faits accomplis* was apparently saved from judicial rebuff by Pearl Harbor. Lincoln invoked his command of the armed forces in emancipating slaves; but besides the tremendous moral underpinnings of that proclamation there was the patent, legally cognizable reality of the Civil War from which he could draw constitutional vindication. In declaring martial law in the face of this real war, Lincoln, in spite of the vagueness of the constitutional requirement, subsequently obtained a ratifying resolution from Congress, as did Eisenhower in 1955 for his unilateral declaration on the defense of the Pescadores and Formosa.

No American president has yet made war on his own people, an act which can take any one of several deceptive forms.

Destroying the human rights of an unarmed population by the use of military force is one form of declaring war on a helpless people. This is what has happened in the Philippines with the imposition of a dictatorship through the device of martial law. It should be of urgent interest to Americans to know how a stable democracy, whose will and substance were Filipino, but whose forms were largely American, was so handily and cleverly subverted with the misuse of a loosely worded constitutional clause.

This clause, article VII, Section Ten, Paragraph (2) of the 1935 Constitution, reads as follows:

> The President shall be Commander-in-Chief of all armed forces of the Philippines and, whenever it becomes necessary, he may call out such armed forces to prevent or suppress lawless violence, invasion, insurrection, or rebellion. In case of invasion, insurrection, or rebellion, or imminent danger thereof, when the public safety requires it, he may suspend the privilege of the *Writ of Habeas Corpus,* or place the Philippines or any part thereof under Martial Law.

The explicit language of this clause immediately sets it fairly far apart from its American model. While the United States Constitution makes the president the

Commander-in-Chief of the Army, Navy, and the State Militia, it vests no one with the power to declare martial law. Also, it is exasperatingly vague even as to who may suspend the writ of *habeas corpus* when "in cases of rebellion or invasion the public safety may require it."

There is no debate over the Philippine president's power—under the stated conditions—to declare martial law without the prior consent of Congress. But two questions must yet be answered. To what extent may the president, under cover of martial law, disturb the civil rights of the people? And may not the courts examine the validity of his proclamation to determine whether the conditions for the imposition of martial law did in fact exist and, furthermore, judge the validity of the acts performed by the government in the name of martial law?

To uncover the answers to these questions we have mostly American statutes and jurisprudence to study, for Philippine jurisprudence, which in the field of constitutional law is of course heavily reliant on American precedents, is particularly barren on this point. The reason is simply that no Philippine Chief Executive, whether an American *civil* governor or a Filipino President, had ever proclaimed martial law before 1972.

However, one American *military* governor did. His name was General Arthur MacArthur, father of Douglas MacArthur. In his book *Mother America* General Romulo is proud to recall that although in 1899 MacArthur "as Military governor ... held the Philippines under Martial Law," he on the other hand "established the writ of *Habeas Corpus,* which is the foundation stone of the American Bill of Rights."

"This," General Romulo aptly observes, "was a daring act in a country still at war." And, we might now add, it was a lesson in restraint from a military governor for his civilian successors.

When the Philippine-American war was over, it was time for the American government to carry out peacefully President McKinley's historic resolve to "civilize" the Filipinos (whose leaders were graduates of Manila universities older than Harvard) and to "Christianize" the Filipino Catholics.

The United States Congress enacted the Philippine bill of 1902 which authorized the President of the United States or the American Governor-General, *not* to declare martial law, but only to suspend the writ of habeas corpus "when in cases of rebellion, insurrection, or invasion the public safety may require it" and only with the consent of the Philippine Commission, which was the nearest thing at the time to a legislative body for the Philippine Government.

In 1916 the Jones Law gave the Governor-General the power to declare martial law under similar conditions, but adding: "or imminent danger thereof." It also subjected his decision to review, modification, or nullification by the President of the United States.

The 1935 Constitution then reproduced this authority in the office of the President of the Philippines, but removed all mention of legislative consent.

The wording is deceptive, for it appears to circumscribe the grant of power to declare martial law with specified conditions that would seem to be reasonably recognizable to the lay mind.

Once the constitutional provision is invoked and the President declares martial law, without having to secure anyone else's consent, must the people accept his unilateral assertion that there is "invasion, insurrection or rebellion, or imminent danger thereof" even if the obvious reality is to the contrary? The president may, of course, claim access to intelligence reports which he cannot reveal in detail without violating the now generously publicized principle of "confidentiality" and so ask the people to bear with him and believe what they cannot see.

Orthodox religious faith, indeed, requires that one believe even in what one cannot see. Yet obviously even the most pious delegate to our 1934 Convention never meant to equate constitutional probity with religious faith. We must also assume that the delegates did not intend to place in the hands of the president the absolute power to destroy the very system which they were carefully designing and for the slightest alteration to which they were devising an elaborate and difficult amending formula.

It must be presumed that the delegates accepted that the recognizable tests found in American constitutional jurisprudence should be applied in answering the question "Is martial law called for?"—regardless of the nature of the conditions under which it might be declared or in whose hands the power to declare it has been constitutionally put.

The delegates were meeting over sixty years after the Supreme Court of the United States had decided the case of *Ex Parte Milligan*. The majority opinion in that celebrated decision had fixed a very simple test: Martial law can be declared only in areas where the civil courts cannot function because of civil disorder.

In the case of *Duncan v. Kahanamoku*, the same court through Justice Black lamented that martial law seemed to have no precise meaning in law. Justice Black went on to warn that neither the federal nor any state or territorial Organic Act could ever be interpreted to permit a form of martial law "contrary to our political philosophy and institutions." We should anticipate parenthetically the evident corollary in this statement: that martial law may not be used to destroy those same institutions.

The Philippine constitutional scholar Irene Cortes in her noted work *The Philippine Presidency* accepts the Milligan and Duncan cases as proper sources of limitations on the Philippine president's power to declare martial law. Philippine Supreme Court Justice and constitutional commentator Enrique Fernando also reminds us that martial law does not imply that military law is substituted for civil law; the proclamation of martial law, he adds, only serves to warn citizens that the military powers have been called upon by the executive to assist him in the maintenance of law and order.

Yet Marcos was not disposed to observe these limitations. Among his first triumphant announcements was that the streets of Manila had been made cleaner and garbage collection was faster. This surely must have driven not a few citizens to reread the constitution to see if they perhaps had a wrong understanding of the conditions for martial law, and whether the constitution might not in fact provide that the president may declare martial law in cases of invasion, insurrection, rebellion, or sluggish garbage collection!

PEACE, DEVELOPMENT, AND LIBERTY

In 1966 Pope Paul VI suggested that "development is the new name for peace." John F. Kennedy did not put it that way, but he did imply the same dynamic thrust when he rallied the youth of America to a Peace Corps of volunteers to work in developing nations.

If peace means development, we must then ask: What is the quality of the peace that development must produce, or better, must accompany? Surely it is not a mute and regimented peace or, to indulge in a cliché, the peace of the grave—a state so quickly attainable by successful war or repression. It is a peace, one would expect, that would go with human dignity.

One of the components of human dignity is *liberty,* and we must now ask: May we, or must we, suppress some of the essence of that dignity in order to help man finally attain it?

In the late 60s in some of the highest academic circles in America, the boast was made that scholarly research had successfully segregated development from liberty, and had proven, in fact, that they might be contradictory.

In 1968, a distinguished political scientist, Samuel Huntington, wrote that this was the "classic dilemma of the first phase of political modernization: traditional pluralism confronts modernizing despotism, liberty is pitted against equality" (*Political Order in Changing*

Societies, New Haven, Yale University Press, 1968, p. 160).

Modernization, whatever that may add up to, is, by implication, equated with development. One is left almost in terror at the thought that some well-meaning libertarians with their incessant chanting about human rights might be spoiling the chances of developing nations by standing in the way of the modernizing despot, who begins to emerge as the last best hope of civilization.

The closest ally of the new modernizing despot is the technocrat—the rationalizer and the planner of the national economy. The first deity in his pantheon is the Gross National Product, and he is not generally patient with systems that allow themselves to be slowed down by the observance of human rights.

In 1970, Alvin Toffler predicted the death of technocracy, of "econo-think," which starts "from the premise that even non-economic problems can be solved with economic remedies." He said that technocratic planning undertaken without popular participation is doomed to failure in developed nations (*Future Shock,* New York, Bantam, 1970, pp. 477 ff.). How then could the less willing masses of the developing nations be badgered into following a plan in which they have had no say?

It is, however, not Toffler's late warning but rather the earlier paeans of the modernizing despot that seem to have gained the ears of the policy makers and international agencies. Like that of the circus barker, the cry became "hurry, hurry, hurry!" Hurry or there will be disaster, urged the President of the World Bank. Development needs stability and order, and these come best with military governments, observed the Rockefeller Report on Latin America.

You must move forward! Democracy is too slow! Human rights can wait!

There is a touch of condescension in this exhortation. But it is full of possibilities for African, Latin American, and Asian politicians with their own private visions of "modernizing despotism."

In the last two decades, whenever an Asian leader, tired of coping with a legal opposition, began to fear the people and decided to run things permanently on his own, he issued a proclamation blaming all his country's ills on "Western-style democracy" and immediately instituted Western-style repression. He imprisoned the opposition, muzzled the press, and silenced the population by putting the fear of pre-dawn military police raids in their hearts—devices terribly western and so terribly effective.

Then, following his secret Western idols, he dressed up the repression with euphemistic terminology. One called it "guided democracy," another "basic democracies," still another his "own road to socialism." The latecomer of the seventies is, of course, Marcos's "New Society."

These self-discovered Asian messiahs did not hesitate to execute Western-style stage-management and buck-passing techniques in preparing for the takeover. Hitler burned the Reichstag and blamed it on the Communists. Marcos bombed the toilet of the Constitutional Convention and blamed it on the Maoists.

The way having been cleared "to get things done," a grand vision of development was announced and then hotly pursued; but soon it became evident that without creative popular initiative it was bringing the country either to stagnation or to a tragic, if spectacular, Western-style *denouement*.

Indonesia's "guided democracy" collapsed in a Teutonic-style bloodbath and her army took over with assurances to the people of an eventual return to parliamentary democracy. Pakistan's "basic democracies" had to be given up to meet the demands of her East wing for the restoration of the parliamentary process, and the West wing's reluctance to accept the consequences of the restoration produced the Balkanization of the country. Burma is bogged down Iberian-style on her own road to socialism and her students and Buddhist monks now are demanding change. The abandonment by Marcos of "Western-style democracy" is challenged with increasing daring by those who still manage to express the will of the people, notably the solid phalanx of eighty-one bishops of that good old-fashioned Western-style institution— the Roman Catholic Church.

Meanwhile, some will continue to go along with the canard that Asians, like Westerners, are indeed capable of repression but, unlike Westerners, are quite incapable of democracy.

We need not belabor the evidence that political and social repression abounds in Western as well as in non-Western history. The whole of human history seems sometimes to read like the unending story of the struggle of man—Western and non-Western—against repression. And the instruments of torture and death devised to persuade or eliminate those unwilling to submit to repression acquire their cruel refinements as exquisitely in medieval England and Spain as they did in early Chinese dynasties.

As for democracy, its direct form practiced in Athens, glorious but imperfect with its freemen *and* slaves, has been called a "brief historical episode" unrelated to the development of modern parliamentary democracy. Plato did not like it and Aristotle was at best tolerant of it. After the decline of Greece, the Western world would not hear of democracy on a national scale again for two thousand years.

The Magna Carta of the thirteenth century was a bill of rights, not of the people, but of the barons against the despot. It was not until the seventeenth century that the British parliament began to evolve away from its oligarchic traditions. It would not be until 1918 that the British would enjoy universal male suffrage, and not until 1928 that their women would be allowed to vote.

Meanwhile, Mexicans will remind us that the Aztecs and Mayans enjoyed a measure of democracy comparable to that in modern constitutional republics. Anthropologists have written that some forms of tribal consensus in Africa are in fact democratic. And Alistair Cooke in his folksy historical essay, *America,* quite categorically affirms that there were democratic as well as totalitarian societies among the original inhabitants of North America before Columbus ever set foot on San Salvador.

In 1966 Barrington Moore, Jr., in his study *Social Origins of Dictatorship and Democracy,* saw the development of democracy as a "long and certainly incomplete struggle to do three closely related things: 1) to check arbitrary rulers, 2) to replace arbitrary rulers with just and rational ones, and 3) to obtain a share for the underlying population in the making of rules."

For his Asian specimen he chose India and found that these three steps had been at least partially taken there; but he also seemed to wonder why Indian democracy with so many imperfections is able to survive at all. Furthermore, he attributed the weakening of the landed aristocracy exclusively to the British occupation and rejected any hint of the capacity of Indian culture and society themselves to develop indigenous democratic institutions.

However, others who have made a more concentrated study of Indian society believe otherwise. Lloyd and

Susan Rudolph in 1967 disputed the Marxian dichotomy between tradition and modernity, which they said stemmed from a "misdiagnosis of tradition and a misunderstanding of modernity." The Rudolphs studied the village consensus and the indigenous laws of India and found them to have been material in the building of a successful Indian democracy. They found that even caste, "that most pervasive and, for most students of Indian society, Marxian and non-Marxian alike, most retrograde of India's social institutions, has not only survived the impact of British imperialism but also transformed and transvalued itself."

They point to the caste associations, which they call paracommunities which pursue social mobility, political power, and economic advantage, not unlike the voluntary associations of interest groups familiar to European and North American politics.

Where caste was absent, village consensus was of course even more effective. In Indonesia it was called *mufakat*, resulting from free discussion called *musjuwarah*. Mohammad Hatta, the former Vice-President of Indonesia, admitted in 1956 that early Indonesia states were feudal and ruled by autocratic kings but "in the villages a democratic system remained in force and lived a healthy life as part and parcel of *adatistiadat*, old usage and traditional custom."

In India, as in Europe, the ownership of land was the foundation of feudal power. But in Indonesia land was the communal property of the village and therefore provided the hedge against the despot that Barrington Moore thinks elemental in the development of a democratic society. Out of this common land power base, the people developed other democratic rights and traditions—the *gotong rojong* or mutual assistance principle, the right to leave the king's realm, the right to make protest against regulations issued by the king, and the right to a general meeting at the village green.

Sometimes, instead of holding a meeting, the villagers would simply squat mutely on the green as a sign that they were not willing to obey a certain edict of the king, thus presaging in remarkably detailed fashion that very democratic and, if you will, Western twentieth-century remedy—the sit-down strike.

So democracy, then, developed within the centralized monarchies of India and Indonesia. But not all Asian nations possess a monarchical tradition.

"Nothing about the early Filipinos," says the historian Horacio de la Costa, "struck the first Spanish settlers, coming as they did from a Europe of centralized monarchies, so much as the fact that they had no kings." Islam, with her sultans and kings, had not yet blanketed the northern and central islands, and Spaniards found settlements which were ruled by chiefs called *datus,* who were not hereditary rulers but who rose to power in one of various familiar ways.

The Jesuit chronicler Colin, describing the process of acquiring this rank, relates that "a man may be of lowly birth but if he exerts himself, if by dint of hard work and shrewdness he accumulates wealth, whether it be by farming or husbandry, whether it be by trade or the practice of some craft known to them, or whether it be by robbery or oppression . . . such a man acquires ascendancy and renown."

Are these not some of the ways, not excluding the last, by which some Western politicians are reported, or reputed, to get into public office today?

What takes shape in these settlements, called *Balangays,* is something dramatically resembling the Greek city state. The chiefs are the nobility and below them are the gentlemen, called *maharlikas,* who paid neither tax nor tribute but who were bound to follow the chief to war; the commoners, called *aliping namamahay,* who were householders who gave half of their farm produce to the lord; and slaves, called *aliping saquiquilir,* who served the lord in his house and could be sold. The chief could rise from any of these estates and his kinsmen did not necessarily rise with him. A *datu* could have a brother or even a son who was a slave. And the land, as in Indonesia, was communally owned.

There emerges here again that elemental democracy—the absence of arbitrariness. The *datu* was no absolute, hereditary, landowning monarch. He rose by consensus, even though sometimes that consensus— as in modern democracies—might have been secured by fraud. It was also a superior democracy in that it was not nepotistic, which should demolish the current argument that the Filipino is not historically predisposed to true democracy because, among other things, he is hopelessly snarled in family ties.

The extreme form in which family ties can engulf the Filipino is the *compadre* system which, as the word implies, and as in Latin America, was not an indigenous but a Spanish cultural infusion, by which family obligations, already abundant by consanguinity and affinity, are expandible *ad infinitum* by the process of sponsorships at the baptismal font. The grotesque distortions in the Italian version of these relationships were depicted for us in Mario Puzo's *The Godfather.*

The Spaniards must also take the responsibility for another reputed Filipino disqualification for democracy, namely, the admitted but often exaggerated incapacity of the millions of land-bound share-cropping tenants to vote independently of their landlords. The Spanish government institutionalized the *datu* into the *Cabeza de*

Barangay and made the office the hereditary instrument of the central government.

The communal lands were transformed into public domain available for private titling by the *Cabezas*, who with their families were constituted into the *principalia*. Thus in one stroke two institutions of the original democracy were destroyed—the rise of the chief by consensus, and the communal character of the land which, as in Indonesia, might have provided the hedge against a central monarch even if that monarch were an alien governor-general. The same stroke produced the landlord-tenant society in the feudal traditions of medieval Europe.

Out of this discussion there surfaces a revisionist commentary on Western colonialism. While it did bring to Asian colonies Western democratic forms, Western colonialism also disturbed the healthy development of truly indigenous democratic institutions. On the other hand, those elements in early Asian society, which if left alone may have evolved into modern indigenous institutions, did not retard, but on the contrary, propelled the development of Asian democracy in borrowed but malleable Western forms.

This is the way it was working in the Philippines. There the native will to democracy, stunted but not killed by Spanish domination, was able to rally the Filipinos in the first successful upheaval against Western colonialism in Asia. The First Republic of 1898 was to have been governed under a constitution, 30 percent of which consisted of a bill of rights. The Americans came, aborted the Republic, and during forty-eight years of occupation sought to atone for the sin of abortion by allowing the Filipinos a measure of democracy unique in colonial annals.

In 1906, the Filipinos, if they were male and literate or

could claim a minimum of property or tax payments, were already voting for national officials. Similar restrictions were at that time also burdened on the British voter. In 1935 universal male and female suffrage were adopted in the new Philippine constitution. This was only eighteen years after British male voters had acquired unrestricted suffrage and seven years after British women had acquired the right to vote.

Philippine democracy had its serious faults and constitutional infirmities. One of these was the magnitude of presidential power, more overwhelming than that in the United States, where it continues to be in the center of critical national debate. The other was an artificial party system by which two political parties were given exclusive protection at the counting of the ballots—a system which prevented the evolution of progressive and conservative alternatives. The social and political imbalance was due largely to these two faults, and in 1972 we were about to correct them in the Constitutional Convention discussed earlier.

Meanwhile, a companion revolutionary development was transpiring in the provinces. The farmers were suddenly meeting with success in organizing themselves into powerful federations, voting independently of their landlords, and delivering an impact on the political institutions. Father Bruno Hicks, an American Franciscan missionary who was expelled by Marcos upon declaration of martial law and who had worked for years with the farmers of Central Philippines, described the phenomenon as "democracy beginning to work."

With the declaration of martial law the "New Society" of Marcos has begun to disintegrate. In September 1974 all the eighty-one Catholic bishops of the Philippines, where Catholicism embraces 86 percent of the population, demanded the end of martial law. The *Washington*

Post later reported that the Archbishop of Manila had called a press conference in which he delivered his latest indictment of the dictatorship on the occasion of the hunger strike begun by the imprisoned publisher of the *Manila Chronicle.* He accused the government of torture and dismemberment of detainees, ruthless suppression of the press, the crushing of the labor movement, and welshing on the promise of land reform. He said, "If the people are not informed properly you can expect them to be cynical about government programs."

Earlier it had been reported that the so-called land reform program could not progress because Marcos had discovered that many of those adversely affected composed the bulwark of his dictatorship—including army officers. In this era, land reform will not succeed by technocratic sloganeering. Those who need the land reform must be free to organize and fight for its implementation. But the right of the farmers to organize and protest was one of the first freedoms to be killed, and many farmer leaders have been imprisoned.

The moral here is that development or modernization, if it is to be fundamental, human, and permanent, cannot be divorced from liberty. Development without liberty rubs violently against the historical and cultural grain of many developing nations, generating tensions and instabilities that threaten peace. These are marks of the Philippines today, where Marcos pretends to govern without a successor. The traditional safety valves of free expression are shut. If anything should happen to Marcos, or if a people tired of high prices, uncertainty, and repression should suddenly erupt in revolt, a chaotic condition would ensue.

Compounded with the stubborn rebellion of the Muslims, who would have been satisfied with substantial constitutional autonomy but were provoked into armed action by martial law, and with the dissidence of the Maoists which would otherwise be manageable, this chaos could suck the large American military and economic presence into another protracted debacle. It would be an easy matter for the Marcos cohorts who engineered the toilet crisis of 1972 to throw bombs into American installations and industrial establishments and blame it all on the Maoists, hoping to involve American forces irrevocably on their side.

The bloodless alternative has to begin with an unequivocal stand by the United States that it is not supporting the Marcos dictatorship. There is precedent for such a disavowal. On October 17, 1972, only three weeks after the Marcos coup, Park Chung Hee declared his own martial law in South Korea. On the same day the *New York Times* reported that the State Department had "conveyed to the South Korean Government in the stiffest terms its disapproval" of Park's sudden move which was a "blow to American policy . . . to assist democratic developments" in that country.

It was different in the Philippines. There, the morning after the Marcos coup, the American Chamber of Commerce sent an enthusiastic telegram of support to the Presidential Palace. Some firm voices of protest have been heard in the U.S. Senate and House of Representatives, in the American press, in the churches and on university campuses. But there is yet no official word of disapproval of the killing of democracy in a country of whose democratic institutions America would so fondly like to claim to be the foster mother. No official voice has yet complained of the imprisonment of thousands of Filipinos whose only crime is to stand up for the ideals proclaimed in the American Constitution, in the Universal Declaration of Human Rights, in the primers and readers taught by American teachers in Philippine public schools.

With this official silence, with continuing U.S. military

aid, with World Bank and multinational corporate enthusiasm, Marcos feels entitled to claim that the United States is in his pocket. And the Filipino people are entitled to believe that he is telling the truth.

An American disavowal would encourage internal forces of peaceful change to move quickly and head off a chaotic explosion. Three important countries have just moved back from dictatorship to democracy with a minimum of bloodshed: Thailand, Portugal, and Greece. They demonstrated once more that the human passion for freedom knows no geographical or racial bounds, and that this passion cannot be stifled by seven, ten, or fifty years of repression even with modern weaponry and techniques. The events in Portugal are showing that the longer the dictatorship is allowed to last, the more difficult the readjustment to democracy becomes. From the experience of these three brave peoples, and with the heavy hand of America relaxed, the Filipinos could distill their own formula for the peaceful return of their lost historic liberties.

When America disengages itself from repression, it might turn its attention to the redirection of its aid programs to serve the cause of development in liberty and, thereby, the cause of peace. America might listen to Americans like George C. Lodge, who proposes that advanced nations take short-term political risks that may yield long-term gains for humanity, by addressing their assistance to what he calls the "engines of change" in the developing nations—the democratic peasant organizations, the labor federations, the movements for peaceful social liberation. It is good to assist land reform programs; it is better to assist forces that will make governments carry them out. It is good to fund industrial projects; it is better to fund the movements that are fighting to form the capital, build the base, and enlarge the market of industry.

Somehow this challenge has a more promising ring than urgent calls for economic growth, for the "enlargement of the pie" without serious concern for civil liberties. One or two European countries have picked up the challenge. As the two hundredth year of America approaches it might be timely to return to the old faith that freedom is still worth taking risks for. The current story of India is not yet finished. All the major crises of the seventies tell us a common message: Democracy is still the wave of the future. The fall of South Vietnam and Cambodia, which were never working democracies, does not invalidate this message.

Sincere Americans may sometimes stand in awe when systems that cannot balance liberty with equality seem to do quite well with equality alone. John Kenneth Galbraith recently visited China and exulted: "I have seen the future and it works." Yet I doubt if he would seriously include in his prescription for the future of developing nations those periodic subcontinental convulsions that are required to keep the Chinese system going, or the countless decapitations that were required to get it started.

Democracy, said Winston Churchill, is the worst form of government, but all other forms are even worse. There is optimism and caution, pride and humility in that cryptic act of faith in the rights of man. But we can ignore it only if we are ready to give up the waging of peace.

ASIAN REVOLUTION AND
AMERICAN IDEOLOGY

Asia wants revolution; Asia needs revolution. The only Asian nation to which this truth does not apply is Japan, whose society was transformed in the nineteenth century. Once all of Asia was in a state of equilibrium, with its agrarian societies relying for survival on a delicate balance between land and population. Land suitable for rice-growing was limited and rice-eating populations struggled for subsistence; they had neither the time, ability, nor energy to think of governing themselves or even of participating in government. The task of governing was left to the few, a small, specialized class of scholar-officials. To labor and obey was left to the many. Thus the centralized state came into being, strong enough to protect these precarious balances from ever-threatening natural or artificial forces, skilled enough to undertake the control of the flow of water, the life-blood of the staple production.

In the centers of Asian culture, in India, Java, Cambodia, Japan and most especially in China, there was strong central government and a statically arranged society. In China, it was a pyramid, the peasants at the bottom, the land-owning gentry above them, still higher the scholar-administrators and at the summit the emperor, the divine maintainer of the equilibrium between land and population, man and nature, heaven and earth.

Confucius gave this stability a philosophic base which sanctified harmony and reverence for authority. But if the balance were disturbed, if the emperor could not control the avarice of landlords, the corruption of officials, the looting by invading babarians, and if therefore the masses starved, the sacred work-cycle stopped and there was chaos, there yet was a remedy: the ruler ceased to be divine. Rebellion was permitted, nay called for, and the successful rebel was by his victory ipso facto vested with divine power. A new dynasty was born and the balance was restored. The Chinese formula was adopted, with modifications, throughout East Asia.

This kind of equilibrium was to last four thousand years, until one day Western man arrived with ideas more explosive than the powder the Chinese had invented for firecrackers at the harvest festival (and which the Westerner would later push into the mouths of cannon). Among these new ideas were Christianity, proclaiming human rights superior to those of the state; science, substituting immutable laws for the capricious will of the gods; parliamentary government, making the governor responsible to the governed; and new techniques for mass production and the control of disease.

Asian society was shaken to its roots. European governors replaced indigenous rulers, and the land once tilled only for the subsistence of the population was now made to produce raw materials for the colonial power.

When the Manchus fell in China, there was no other dynasty to take their place. The cluster of Western ideas, which the Europeans had never bothered to knit together into one harmonious whole to replace the old Asian equilibrium, fell on Asian ground as separate elements, breeding hope and despair in expectations that could not soon be fulfilled. Mass populations grew, unchecked by the old natural levellers, plague and epidemic; plantation economies stagnated because they were geared to export crops whose markets had faded away with the departure of the colonials.

Asia is left today with more ambition and less fulfillment, more people and less food. The equilibrium is gone. And no new rebel can assume the divine mantle and restore the harmony. The Asian, converted to the ideas of the West, now wants to control his government and his destiny. Though he may still be at the base of the old pyramid he wants dignity for himself—not just for the emperor, the potentate or the scholar-official, and not just for the native aristocrat or the *comprador*.

This now is the question: Is America ready to face the necessity of revolution? Many Americans would probably find the question impertinent. Are they not the first revolutionaries of the modern age? Is not their Declaration of Independence a ringing revolutionary document for men of all time to invoke in the cause of justice and equality?

They are, indeed, entitled to be proud. But recalling one's own revolution is perhaps not enough, or at least is a different thing from understanding another's hunger for revolutionary change. It becomes even less adequate when America's original revolution and its ideological underpinnings no longer seem relevant to the deep current of human events where men now need revolution most—among the masses of the developing world.

In another era, one of limited population and pure libertarian motives, the American Revolution was surely relevant. When America snatched independence from the first Philippine Republic at the turn of the century, William Jennings Bryan replied to the imperialists' justification of "educating the Filipinos": The educated Filipinos are now in revolt against us, and the most ignorant ones have made the least resistance to our domination. If we are to govern them without their consent and give them no voice in determining the taxes which they must pay, we dare not educate them, lest they learn to read the Declaration of Independence and Constitution of the United States and mock us for our inconsistency.

But the reasoning of John Locke and the precepts of Isaac Newton, which were the wellsprings of the principles of the American Constitution and Declaration of Independence, seem to have little bearing on questions like the pressures of population, the closing of the breach between rich and poor, the rapid demolition of the barriers of race and creed.

Equality is good, but in the newly emerging nations there is now too much equality in destitution. Dignity would be better. But where in the "rockets' red glare" of the American Revolution can we see how this dignity may be won by the multiplying millions of this age? In a world searching for an ideology that will bestow this dignity, where even the youth of America seeks a "national purpose," America's only answer seems to be pragmatic improvisation, meeting crises on a "case-to-case" basis.

And all the while, Americans are unpragmatically espousing or rejecting ideas because of associations that are either imprecise or no longer applicable. The idea of capitalism is a primary example. America is a monument to the genius of free enterprise and American propagandists abroad would like to credit her unabated economic growth to completely free initiative, almost to classic laissez-faire.

This is what the young Filipino entrepreneur, inspired by the American example, schooled in the American tradition and seeking to build his enterprise in the American image, is told when he seeks assistance from the Philippine government in order to compete with the giant American firms operating freely within the uncontrolled Philippine economy. No mention is made of American government controls and subsidies that enable the "free-enterprise" economy to accommodate the concern for the national welfare.

Americans are proud to be known as alert opponents of socialism, yet poll-takers report that millions of Western Europeans, Asians, Africans and Latin Americans think of themselves as "socialists," and that this "socialism" is much akin to what the Americans themselves believe in. (*Cf.* Ralph K. White, " 'Socialism' and 'Capitalism': An International Misunderstanding," *Foreign Affairs,* January 1966) Americans are proud of their crusading anti-Communism. Yet to many in the uncertain world, Communism is opposed to capitalism, not to democracy.

Even America's allies and non-Communist friends are beginning to tire of negative anti-Communism. As early as 1963, Don Van Sung, the Vietnamese patriot, warned: "By emphasizing anti-Communism rather than positive revolutionary goals and from lack of a better adaptation to the local situation, the United States has reduced its anti-Communist efforts in Viet Nam to the maintenance of an administrative machine and of an army." To Eduardo Frei, the former Christian Democratic President of Chile, "the anti-Communisms of fear, of preservation of 'order,' and of forces manifested in military coups are doomed to failure and are constantly in rout. They have nothing to say to youth or the people."

But, it will be asked, what need is there of ideology? Did not pragmatism cure the ills of America? We may largely agree. The histories of other nations are always divided into periods of rise and decay, of benevolent kings and lecherous kings, of the ascendancy of reason and the rise of faith, of progress and reaction. American history is singularly lacking in these periods and in this respect it is monotonous. But it is the unique, consistent and gloriously monotonous American condition which accounts for the fact that every minute an American is born free, free in every sense, to develop himself and his country according to his own will and initiative.

There will never be one single man known as the builder of America. And this just might be America's guarantee for greatness without end, for escaping the cycle of rise and fall which some historians predict for great civilizations. What shall we call this guarantee? Capitalism? Free enterprise? We might more aptly use the word which a hard-headed monk of the thirteenth century once associated with freedom. Thomas Aquinas said that "freedom is the spontaneous obedience to law." Spontaneity may be the key. And as America built itself spontaneously, so also could we build Asia.

But Asia is not ready for spontaneity. There is at present little enthusiam in Asia for the American example; for it is apparent that patchwork democracy requires conditions which do not exist in the developing world. One such condition is the challenge of the open frontier—the response to which was the beginning of the American miracle. There are no such frontiers to challenge Asians. The Asian peasant must respond not to the heartening call of the rich wild but to the demoralizing prospect of having to make productive two hectares of unowned land, his tenancy having emanated from some unwritten ancestral contract or royal decree which his ancestor could not read.

This absence of Asian frontiers has moved practical theologians like Ceylonese Oblate Father Tissa

Balasuriya to urge that the developed white countries abounding in virgin land, such as Canada, Australia and the United States, voluntarily give way to the demands of "macro-justice" and open their frontiers to the land-hungry millions of Asia. Writing in *Commonweal* (December 24, 1965), he says, "If I were born of white parents almost the entire under-inhabited world would be open to me to settle down and reproduce my kind—Australia, Canada, South Africa, Southern Rhodesia, etc. . . . Yet these same countries generously give non-whites arms to fight the Communists to make the world safe for political democracy and 'Christian civilization.' And they blame us when we are not enthusiastic. The present policy of 'increase and multiply and stay where you are, for we have filled the earth' cannot, humanly speaking, last." This may sound extreme to some, but it helps explain why most Asians will not find inspiration in the squirrel-capped figure of Daniel Boone.

A second condition, native to, but later blunted in Asia is the American tradition of dissent. The very act of crossing the Atlantic by the original American settlers was one of dissent—dissent from oppression, from tyranny, simple dissent from opposing opinion. The waves of Malays and Proto-Malays that landed on the shores of Luzon, Visayas, and Mindanao, the early Filipinos (who drove the Negritos and Igorots away from the lowlands and into the mountain fastnesses just as the early Americans were later to drive the indigenous population eventually into reservations) came in groups of families called *balangays*. These men were no fugitives from tyranny, but their tradition was free consensus—consensus under the leadership of the chief or *datu*, who rose to office also by consensus. But soon it would be conformism to the will of the white colonial governor.

Nonconformism would cease to be a right, and the penalty for it would invariably be heavy.

There is yet a third condition—the richness of the land. The pioneers found in the American continent a prodigious wealth of resources. Indeed there are pockets of great natural wealth in parts of Asia, not excluding the Philippines. But most Asians work barren land and must overcome superstition before putting to use the fertilizer that will fatten the soil.

No wonder, then, that Asia is ready for freedom but not yet ready to understand spontaneity. No wonder that some Asians are confused, for it is quite possible that something akin to American spontaneity can come from other antecedents. The Filipino writer Nick Joaquin reported after a visit to Red China that "responsiveness to challenges is the spirit that is Americanizing the Chinese." He says that the party line this year in New China sounds like Babbitt at a salesmen's pep talk: "Go all out, aim high, get results! Think big! Act big!" What could be more "Damn Yankee?" he asks. "If you bumped into it in the dark, could you guess this was Chinese, not Rotarian; that this was Slave State, not Rugged Individualism?"

Responsiveness without freedom. Is this paradox really possible? If it is, it is the result of an upheaval the premises of which have been easier for Asians to understand: The simple dichotomy of the rich and the poor, the oppressor and the oppressed, the few and the many. The rich are the few, the poor are the many. Let the many rise in revolution and redistribute the fruits of the earth—this is something Asians may understand, a revolution an Asian may indeed find easy to join, because he knows the poverty, the inequality, the oppression and all the rest. It is certainly easier to join than that complicated revolt against stultifying tradition, that rebellion against self through which he would have to go before he could enjoy the privilege of "pragmatic" spontaneity.

This is not to say that Americans are incapable of magnificent responses to challenges that excite other men and other nations. The whole history of America is a sequence of such performances—much like the improvisations of a jazz band, with each instrumentalist going his own individual way and still contributing to a totality that is a smashing success. But for Asians, what chance has such a performance, however brilliant, against the sustained, persistent, unequivocal panorama of revolution projected from other capitals? America is perfectly capable of lighting torches and men will at times follow, but as Jacques Maritain has put it, "for lack of adequate ideology, her lights cannot be seen. I think," he adds, "it is too much modesty."

Call it modesty, call it indifference, call it overconfidence; whatever it may be, I do not suggest that America stop lighting torches, for even though they may not last, they will always be useful in the dark. But America could also light a beacon, project a permanent beam steadily proclaiming what she stands for and informing the peoples of the world what it is they might gain from her leadership in the elevation of each human life.

Americans are almost organically averse to traditional ideology. This aversion may have been fitting to the early American, but how proper is it to the modern American—the American with a global commitment to leadership? Unless it is his desire to withdraw into isolation, he must collect his bundle of brilliant improvisations and distill from them an ideology relevant to the problems of this age and the lives of those millions who are touched by his commitment.

It is up to the Americans to draw the ideological possibilities out of their pragmatic experience, but an Asian is perhaps entitled to a few expressions of hope. He hopes that the beacon will show the way to a sustained social revolution that will lift men to a level where they may begin to enjoy the freedom and the privilege to be spontaneous. He also hopes this ideology will enable Americans to give better reasons than they have so far given for needed changes. Land must be redistributed because "it is the absolute right of the proletariat," says *Das Kapital;* "because of the social character of property," says *Quadragesimo Anno.* "Because without land reform American aid is wasted," says the American. Will Americans always limit themselves so?

Should we wonder that a man like President Senghor of Senegal, rejecting the scientific socialism of Marx, now turns not to Thomas Jefferson and "life, liberty and the pursuit of happiness," but to Pierre Teilhard de Chardin and his humanistic, optimistic, Christ-centered synthesis of all races evolving irresistibly toward a transcendent God as the hope for *négritude,* for Africa and for mankind? If Africans now turn to Teilhard instead of Jefferson, it is not because the Jeffersonian declaration was not valid. Perhaps because it was so valid and so successful in America, the young and vibrant civilization that it engendered never bothered to review its relevance to the world.

An Englishman has said: "The trouble with Americans is that they want to be on top of the world and still expect to be loved. It simply can't be done, you know."

Is this true, or not? When America has shown the world how she can leap over her barriers of race, of creed, of poverty—not "case-to-case" but by the propulsion of ideas so universal, so understandable that they reach the hearts of all people—who knows? Americans may yet manage to be on top of the world and be loved.

But that is not the important thing. Even without reward for the work of world leadership, there is enough return in the urgency and value of flinging in the teeth of those who create an anonymous and faceless society the idea of a world of people endowed with individual dignity.

The first false god to be toppled in the Asian revolution is paternalism. The family of young nations wants no more of the father image. Max Lerner has pointed out that in the days when American nationalism was taking shape, the Americans first had to slay the European father so that they could then without inhibition use the European heritage in their own drive to greatness. The Indians had to slay the British father to work out their own destiny through British constitutional traditions. The young Filipino entrepreneur must either slay the American father image or at least cut it down to brotherly size so that he can collaborate or compete on equal terms—using the techniques of the Harvard Business School. The Filipino leader must also slay the image so that he can lead his country without self-consciousness to its own version of American constitutional democracy and negotiate treaties with America on the basis of mutual respect.

We are told we need not worry that the Americans will resist the slaying of an image which so ill befits them. A leader among equals, yes, but not a paternalist—not the American with his passion for brotherhood, his sporting blood that will preclude his taking advantage.

So let there be social revolution. Let it fight injustice, give hope. Let it produce wealth, but also close the gap between those who enjoy the wealth and those who do not. Let it not surrender to the simplistic idea that the only problem in Asia is productivity, "the enlarging of the pie," and that the exploitation of man by man will resolve itself with this enlargement. Let it persevere until

the millions of Asia are released from the bonds of retarding traditions, feudal tenancy, and centralized
power. Let America help to fire it, but do not make it an
American revolution. Let it be so universal in meaning,
so pregnant with hope for all races, that each nation will
take it for its own.

MANIFEST
DESTINY

PREFACE

Yes, there are fictional characters in this play. Consul Oscar Williams may have had a daughter like Emilie, but there are no available records to prove it. But Emilie is a character developed to provide a romantic lead, and she serves to articulate stubbornly, if naively, the emerging American conscience in her time.

The only other fictional characters are Carson and O'Malley, the turn-of-the-century models of the American high pressure salesman, spearheading the implementation of the grand design of American expansionism.

Certain liberties have also been taken with two historical characters. It cannot be established that Consul Williams stayed on in Manila to serve as assistant to the Military Governor, although this is a reasonable possibility. And Lieutenant Brumby certainly was not aide to the Secretary of the Navy before he served as Flag Lieutenant to Dewey, performing, as in the play, the role of liaison officer with the Filipino revolutionaries and the defeated Spanish Army. His resignation of his commission to serve as teacher in the "Peace Army" and his romance with Emilie are fictional but prophetic. Many young Americans were later to spurn military service and find fulfillment and romance in the Peace Corps or in movements of protest against oppressive wars.

The rest is history. This is no pompous hyperbole. Others may readily agree with the European dramatist who is reputed to have remarked that "God writes lousy theater." It is not any innate religiosity that moves me to challenge this diminution of God's attributes. I do not feel that I indulge in grandstand modesty when I admit to the feeling that I did not really write this play. I "looked it up," as it were (mostly at the Cornell University library), organized it a bit, and there it was.

An amazing amount of dialogue and song verses will be found to be verbatim transcriptions from Theodore Roosevelt's correspondence with Cabot Lodge, Dewey's official reports, Mahan's writing, Beveridge's speeches, Strong's sermons, and the ringing perorations of William Jennings Bryan. Bryan's "Cross of Gold" piece was delivered before a Democratic National Convention in 1896 and not, as in the play, as a field campaign speech in 1900. But he did bring up the gold issue again in 1900, and it is probable he reiterated the phrase over and over again in the process of diluting the issue of imperialism and losing the election to President McKinley.

It is the authentic account of McKinley's words describing his heavenly vision to the visiting Methodist ministers at the White House that fell most quickly into place as verses for a song. Except for a few alterations to fit the rhyming, his relation, in cadence and pace, fitted perfectly a melody I had put together years ago for a campaign song for the late revered President Ramon Magsaysay of the Philippines. After a moment of prayerful apology to his immortal spirit I decided he would not mind if I found new use for it for a cause he would certainly have espoused today.

Roosevelt's five instructions to the U.S. fleets in the absence of the Secretary of the Navy are sung with almost no alteration. The lines in the scene of the Battle of

Manila Bay, down to the last brash remarks of the ex-boxer Purdy (and Dewey's hilarious post-battle verbal exchange with the German admiral, which made headlines in New York), hew very closely to the report by *New York Herald* correspondent Joseph L. Stickney, whom Dewey had cleverly made his aide.

The verses to elaborate that most nonchalant of all military commands "You may fire when you're ready, Gridley" and for that condescending Kipling injunction "Take up the white man's burden" are contrived but will, I hope, be found to be very much in the spirit of each occasion. The publication of Kipling's poem is here somewhat "advanced" by only a few months (Roosevelt did get an advance copy but not until early 1899) in order to be available for reference at the Hong Kong Club affair tendered by the British in honor of Dewey's staff, an occasion mentioned by Dewey in his autobiography.

Those who may find Stickney's report of the Dewey victory too idealized might find relief in the remarks by a British officer referring to "a hasty gathering of helpless old derelicts" and Emilie Williams' later comment about "sinking helpless navies." Dewey's own official report did reveal a fairly large advantage of fire-power on the part of his squadron.

I am confident our Cuban friends will not resent Dewey's assertion, contained in his official reports, that the Filipinos were better prepared than the Cubans to run an independent government. Dewey after all was not a political scientist. Unlike Douglas MacArthur, he never had the political experience of a governing pro-consul (although MacArthur, like Dewey, overestimated the persuasive value of military victories in obtaining nominations as candidate to the Presidency). Filipinos and Cubans were equally prepared and, like all nations, equally deserving of independence, but it probably

bothered Dewey's subsconscious that the Cubans were to
be given their independence but not the Filipinos.

The scene between General Aguinaldo and Consul
General Pratt in Singapore is reconstructed mostly from
Aguinaldo's own narration in his book *A Second Look At
America*, written when he was far into the autumn of his
life (he died at 93). He insists on his earlier claim that
Pratt had promised him American support for Philippine independence. Whether or not Pratt was authorized
by Dewey (who denied it in a Congressional investigation) or the U.S. Government to make that promise is a
subject that historians will continue to debate and will
probably never settle.

Had I not survived the Japanese war, I would have
passed away with an uncomplicated image of America in
my heart. It would have been the America my American
Jesuit teachers had unveiled to me—of fair play, of liberty with some license, but with even more of what
Thomas Aquinas had called "spontaneous obedience to
law." It would also have been the America (as Theodore
Roosevelt predicts in this play) of Douglas MacArthur
promising to return and put our country back on the
road to democracy.

Had I not survived the cold war of the 1950s I would
also have gone with a still uncomplicated image of
America—this time the America of shining jet armor,
dotting the globe with her invincible bases in order to
defend democracy against the satanic hordes of communism.

But I did survive those wars and I am now in America
in exile, thanks to the hospitality and kindness of friends
and friendly institutions. As I write this, democracy in my
country is gone, but the U.S. bases are still there. And I
ask myself, what are these bases defending the Philippines against now? What on earth is there left to defend
in the Philippines with American lives?

In my exile, I have had the leisure to reflect, to look back, to review the roots of the "special relationships" between the United States and the Philippines. The roots, after just a few scratchings into the soil of history, are there for all to see. They lie in the original vision of Manifest Destiny.

One wonders whether, after almost thirty years of independence, the Philippines has succeeded in graduating from the role of pawn on the chessboard of American ambitions. The withdrawal from Vietnam has placed the Philippines, by admission of American military commanders, in the front line of the American peripheral defense.

Why, after all these bitter realities, do I end this play with high optimism? It is not simply in response to some unwritten law that modern musical plays must end "on the upbeat." It is that after over two years of American exile, if I have gotten to recognize the realities of American policy, I have also gotten to recognize the American people even better. A people that can be hospitable to a foreigner who is critical of their government's policy, to twist W.C. Field's cryptic allusion to persons who hate children and dogs, "can't be all that bad." Such a people, in fact, must be a great people.

This active, aggressive tolerance in America is one of several reasons why the French writer Jean-François Revel once declared that the United States is the only society on earth capable of cradling global social revolution. This is the vision that, with historical license, I have written into the final lines of the enigmatic Theodore Roosevelt. Cynics, observing today's American politics, may scoff at this vision. But I will play the prophet and predict that America will solve her current problems without the sacrifice of human liberties.

Manifest Destiny was first produced in July 1974 in Honolulu, Hawaii, by a group of professors and graduate students of the University of Hawaii and citizens of Honolulu, under the sponsorship of the Filipino Volunteers in Hawaii and the State Council on Philippine Heritage with the following cast and production staff:

COMPANY
(in the order of appearance)

Paul Cravath	Richard Umil	Clint Claussen
Bob Cahill	Bruce Allender	Steve Knoll
Ken Thern	Ted Fritschel	Jim Primm
Mike Forman	Joan Gossett	Tad Gasinski
Clyde Simon	Atiq Khan	George Hudes

Staging Conceived and Directed by   Tomas C. Hernandez
Slide Sequences Prepared and Executed by
    Daniel P. De Castro
Costumer   Peggy Egbert
Musical Arrangement/Pianist   David Kay
Overture Composed by   Angel Peña
Song: *Is it Possible?* music by   Francis Xavier Manglapus
Song: *You Must Open Your Eyes* music by   Tomas C. Hernandez
Drummer   Romarico Flores
Original Cartoons by   Corky Trinidad
Cartoons adapted from *T.R. in Cartoon,*
    (R. Gros, ed.) by   Ludovico Salazar

PRODUCTION STAFF

Production Manager   Malaya Castro
Promotions and Publicity   Inez Cruz, Sheila Forman,
    Bob Stauffer
Poster/Program Design   Fred Yap
Tickets   Dory Yap
Food Committee   Josie Clausen, Chairperson;
                Lina Agbayani, Sumi Chan,
                Mimi Paz, Irma Peña, Charity Quimpo
Assistants to the Costumer   Sumi Chan, Joan Gossett, Nida Greene,
                Irma Peña
House Manager   Amy Cahill
Clean-up Committee   Tabby Cahill, Brownie and Moses Hudes

THE TIME

The winter of 1898 to the winter of 1902

THE SCENES

ACT ONE

Scene 1   The office of the Secretary of the Navy in Washington, D. C.

Scene 2   "The Mansion," a public house on River Valley Road in a suburb of Singapore

Scene 3   The Hong Kong Club

Scene 4   The forward deck of the *U.S.S. Olympia*

Scene 5   The same as Scene 4

Scene 6   Kawit, Cavite

ACT TWO

Scene 1   Fort Santiago in the Walled City of Manila

Scene 2   The same as Scene 1

Scene 3   The office of President McKinley at the White House

Scene 4   An American army forward command post near the bridge of San Juan in the outskirts of Manila

Scene 5   The American front lines in Central Luzon

Scene 6   An open air meeting in the 1900 Presidential campaign

Scene 7   At the gangplank of the transport *U.S.S. Thomas,* just docked at Manila

Scene 8   The front yard of a nipa house in a barrio in Central Luzon

Scene 9   The outer office of the American Military Governor in Manila

Scene 10   The office of President Theodore Roosevelt at the White House

CHARACTERS

(in order of appearance)

NARRATOR

THEODORE ROOSEVELT	Assistant Secretary of the Navy, later Vice-President then President of the United States
HENRY CABOT LODGE	U.S. Senator from Massachusetts
LIEUTENANT THOMAS F. BRUMBY	Junior Aide to Secretary of the Navy Long, later on Dewey's staff
JOSIAH STRONG	Minister, Congregational Church of Cincinnati
ALFRED T. MAHAN	Admiral, naval historian and tactician, instructor, U.S. Naval War College
ALBERT J. BEVERIDGE	U.S. Senator from Indiana
EMILIE WILLIAMS*	Daughter of Consul Williams
E. SPENCER PRATT	U.S. Consul General in Singapore
HOWARD W. BRAY	Englishman, former resident of the Philippines
EMILIO AGUINALDO	Leader of the Philippine Revolution, later President of the Philippine Republic

*FICTIONAL CHARACTER

GREGORIO DEL PILAR	Colonel (later General) of the Philippine Revolutionary Army, aid to Aguinaldo

BRITISH OFFICERS

AMERICAN OFFICERS

GEORGE DEWEY	Commodore, Commander of the U.S. Asiatic Squadron, later rear-Admiral then Admiral of the Navy, U.S. Navy
OSCAR WILLIAMS	U.S. Consul in Manila
ROUNCEVILLE WILDMAN	U.S. Consul General in Hong Kong
JOSEPH L. STICKNEY	Correspondent of the *New York Herald*, Annapolis graduate, appointed acting aide by Dewey
COMMANDER B.P. LAMBERTON	Chief of Dewey's Staff
LIEUTENANT C.P. REES	Executive Officer, Dewey's Staff
LIEUTENANT C.G. CALKINS	Navigator
PURDY	A "privileged" veteran U.S. sailor
CAPT. C.V. GRIDLEY	Captain of the *U.S.S. Olympia*, flagship of the Asiatic Squadron
OTTO VON DIEDERICHS	Vice-Admiral, Commander of the German Asiatic Squadron

GERMAN OFFICERS

FERMIN JAUDENES   Spanish Governor and
                                   Captain-General of the
                                   Philippines

COL. WHITTIER   U.S. Army Colonel, aide to
                                   Gen. Merritt, first com-
                                   mander of U.S. expedi-
                                   tionary force to the Philip-
                                   pines

WILLIAM MCKINLEY   President of the United
                                   States

MINISTERS

SOLDIERS

SENATOR RAWLINS

SENATE INVESTIGATION COMMITTEE

CHARLES S. RILEY   Witness from the 26th
                                   Volunteer Infantry

WILLIAM LEWIS SMITH   Witness from the 26th
                                   Volunteer Infantry

GENERAL ROBERT P. HUGHES   Brig. General, U.S. Army,
                                   Provost Marshall General
                                   of the Philippines

JANUARIUS MANNING   Witness from the 26th
                                   Volunteer Infantry

WILLIAM J. GIBBS   Witness from the 26th
                                   Volunteer Infantry

MAJOR GENERAL ELWELL S. OTIS   Military Governor of the
                                   Philippines

COL. ARTHUR L. WAGNER	Asst. Adjutant General, U.S. Army
FREDERICK FUNSTON	Brig. General, U.S. Army
GENERAL ARTHUR MACARTHUR	Major General, U.S. Army, Military Governor of the Philippines
WILLIAM JENNINGS BRYAN	Democratic Candidate for President, U.S. Senator from Illinois
U.S. CAMPAIGN AUDIENCE	
U.S. SCHOOLTEACHERS	
BILL CARSON*	Salesman
JACK O'MALLEY*	Salesman

MUSICAL NUMBERS

ACT ONE

Scene 1

"The Will! The Will!"	Theodore Roosevelt and Lt. Brumby
"Five Instructions; The American Marco Polo"	Roosevelt and Henry Cabot Lodge
"The Anglo-Saxon Attributes"	Rev. Josiah Strong

Scene 3

"Take Up the White Man's Burden"	Brumby, British Officers, and Emilie Williams
"Williams, Wildman, and Pratt"	Commodore George Dewey

Scene 4

"You May Fire When You're Ready, Gridley"	Dewey

Scene 5

"The Will! The Will!" (reprise)	Dewey, Admiral von Diederichs, American and German Officers

ACT TWO

Scene 1

"What a Way To Deceive Her, España"	Governor-General Jaudenes

Scene 2

"You Must Open Your Eyes"	Emilie

Scene 3

"Civilize and Christianize"   President William McKinley
and Ministers

Scene 4

"Two Dollars a Head!"   Joseph Stickney and Soldiers

Scene 5

"Damn, Damn, Damn   Soldiers and Brumby
the Filipino"

Scene 6

"Marrying Late's Patriotic"   Commander Lamberton, Lt. Rees,
and Stickney

Scene 7

"Is It Possible?"   Emilie and Brumby

Scene 9

"Give a Man a Fish"   Carson, O'Malley, Emilie,
and Brumby

Scene 11

"Those People Make   Roosevelt, Lodge and Brumby
Me Sick!"

"The Will! The Will!"   Roosevelt, Lodge, Emilie, and
(reprise)   Brumby

"Is It Possible?"   Emilie and Brumby
(reprise)

MANIFEST DESTINY

PROLOGUE

NARRATOR: In 1898 Theodore Roosevelt launched the United States on the decisive stage of its Manifest Destiny and the Philippines became the first chosen instrument of that destiny. In the original vision of Manifest Destiny, the Filipinos were not the partners but the pawns. The Filipinos were first used to destroy the Spanish Army and then they themselves had to be destroyed, "pock-marked khakiak ladrones," as the derisive army song went, in order to provide America with raw materials for her industry, buyers for her products, and a gateway to the China trade. In the process, the American conscience rebelled; it was repulsed by the driving vision of markets and glory, and by the hypocritical explanation that all this exploitation was done with the noble ideal of benevolence. Today, we hear no more rhetoric about saving the Philippines—and the world—for democracy. The new shibboleth is stability. Never mind if it is a brittle stability erected by suppressing liberties and plugging the safety valves of free expression. American aid will continue to flow into any country that will serve U.S. interests, a policy no different from the *realpolitik* of other powers.

Despite these bitter realities of American policy, the American conscience, like the Emilies and Brumbys of our play, will make her return to her original ideals and stop subsidizing the killing of those liberties in other lands.

ACT ONE

Act One, Scene 1

NARRATOR: The office of the Secretary of the Navy in Washington, D.C. Time: February 25, 1898, early afternoon. The assistant Secretary of the Navy, THEODORE ROOSEVELT, at the desk. HENRY CABOT LODGE, Senator from Massachusetts, enters.

ROOSEVELT: Cabot!

LODGE: Theodore! (*they embrace*) I looked in on your office, but . . .

ROOSEVELT: But you find me here instead. I was hoping you would come. Now at last I am with someone who will appreciate the meaning of this afternoon. Cabot, Long is absent and I am Acting Secretary. That is why I am using his office.

LODGE: Theodore, splendid! Do you think this might be a good time to . . .

ROOSEVELT: Say no more, Cabot (*buzzes for the Junior Aide*). I'll do it! I'll take the first step in the American march to destiny!

NARRATOR: NAVY LIEUTENANT THOMAS F. BRUMBY, Junior Aide to Long.

BRUMBY: *(enters left and comes stiffly to attention)* I beg your pardon, Sir, I thought . . .

ROOSEVELT: Senator Lodge of Massachusetts, Mr. Brumby. At ease, Mr. Brumby. It's quite all right. Secretary Long is not coming this afternoon. Needs the rest, I think. He's left me in charge. I am Acting Secretary.

BRUMBY: Aye, aye, sir.

ROOSEVELT: Aye, everyone should go home and rest once in awhile. Give things a chance to happen. Let others have a turn at the helm, as it were . . . others . . . with a better sense of history.

BRUMBY: Sir?

LODGE: He said history, my boy, history! This is the afternoon we loosen the chains of history and allow her to run her destined course.

ROOSEVELT: We have reined her in too long, too long *(chuckles)*—heh—no pun intended *(he rises to look through the window through which the Capitol dome is visible)*. Those politicians! They know that war is inevitable. But they have no will to war. There is no will in the Capitol. There is no will at the White House. By George, Brumby, we will give them that will.

(sings and recites)

Refrain:

> *The will! The will! The will to go and fight!*
> *The will! the will—to set the world aright!*

> *There is no place in our world for nations meek as cattle*

Who hesitate to fly the burning standards into battle;
There is no race that can survive by standing soft
*   and courteous*
While others pass it by in hot pursuit of fighting virtues!

You may be skilled in commerce, in art, finance, or science
Or empty oratory—like William Jennings Bryan's;
But you'll never be of greatness and of progress a
*   progenitor*
If you attend to weaklings like George F. Hoar,
*   the Senator;*

Peace may be a victory to Bryan and Hoar,
There is no triumph more supreme than what is
*   won in war!*

(BRUMBY joins in duet)

The will! The will! The will to go and fight!
The will! The will—to set the world aright!

ROOSEVELT: Mr. Brumby do you realize what kind of a
world we would be in if the conquering races in
history had gone against their proud masterful in-
stincts and lost their vigorous hardiness and manli-
ness? Why, sir, civilization would have atrophied!
We might all still be living in the stone age! It is war,
sir, war that is the ideal condition of human society.
It is war that suppresses barbarism and spreads
civilizations. Why, sir . . .

(sings and recites)

How else could slower races whose cultures are inferior
Be blessed with all the benefits achieved by the
*   superior?*
How else can peace be possible unless the stronger
*   carry on*
The fight for subjugation of all the world barbarian?

All this incisive wisdom has obviously been lost on
Those damned anti-imperialists from upper middle
*   Boston!*
They'd make a dirty word out of that chaste
*   centrifugal impulse,*
They'd treat a growing nation like a baby girl
*   with dimples!*

Peace may be a victory to Bryan and to Hoar,
There is no triumph more supreme than what is
*   won in war*

(BRUMBY joins in duet)

The will! The will! The will to go and fight!
The will! The will—to set the world aright!

ROOSEVELT: Mr. Brumby, did you have a course at the academy on the history of empires?

BRUMBY: Well, sir, we did study the relationship between the development of naval tactics and the rise of mercantile protectionism.

ROOSEVELT: That is not exactly what I meant. But after all perhaps there really is no need for a subject on the history of empires. History, just plain history is enough. For without the thrust of empire what sort of world history would we have? Just a series of disconnected vignettes of sterile little cultures withering on the vine.

(sings and recites)

Where would we now be, Brumby, had no one thought
*   to plan*
The process that would civilize the stubborn race
*   called man*

The foolish may shout, "peace, peace," until the
    throat is hoarse,
I say you cannot civilize without the use of force!
Why, Brumby—
In twenty-six hundred B.C.
It was Lugal-Zaggisi
Who first began activities imperial;
A hundred tribes asunder
He forced to buckle under
And civilization thus was born Sumerial!

His glory methods merited
Disgust—but we inherited,
A blessing from this man 'ere he was smitten down—
Lest they babel as in the Bible
He made their speech non-tribal,
Their common language was the first one written down!

    (BRUMBY joins in duet in all refrains)

The will! The will! The will to go and fight!
The will! The will—to set the world aright!

Then came the old king Sargon
Who polished Lugal's jargon
In his semitic empire he named Akkad;
He made the writing uniform
With simple, wedgy cuneiform
(Although today it's rather hard to crack it)!

And there was Hammurabi
The emperor of Baby—
lon whose bloody ways were later modified;
He turned irenic pigeon,
Gave justice and religion,
His statutes were the first in getting codified!

The will! The will! The will to go and fight!
The will! The will—to set the world aright!

And how about the Pharaohs
Those legendary heroes
Whose pyramids have left a vast impression;
When they couldn't beat the Hittite
They cleverly chose to sit tight
And signed the earliest pact of non-aggression!

That truly liberal version
Of colonial rule—the Persian
Whose vassals, though not quite a free electorate,
Were granted such autonomy
(And some free-trade economy)
They'd put to shame the British-style protectorate!

The will! The will! The will to go and fight!
The will! The will—to set the world aright!

Now Philip, King of Macedon,
His mantle soon was passed on
To Alexander, child of the Acropolis,
Who used up all his war money
That men may live in harmony
Together in a Grecian built Cosmopolis;

Alexander died before he
Could reach this crowning glory
And left the task for Romans to persist in,
Whose conquests were heroic,
Whose philosophy was Stoic
So noble it was almost like the Christian!

The Roman was idealist
But also was a realist
He knew that peace was not some ripe banana
You pluck from some blithe tree top
You have to fight and git up—
He fought—and gave the world his Pax Romana!

The will! The will! The will to go and fight!
The will! The will—to set the world aright!

In India the great Asoka
Who wasn't a bit mediocre
Destroyed his foes and then communed in silence;
He then preached peaceful living
And brotherly forgiving;
You see, we must have war before non-violence!

And last, if you'll excuse us,
We can't forget Confucius
Whose people and their culture are a riddle;
They conquered half their neighbors,
Then resting from their labors
Proclaimed themselves the Kingdom of the Middle!

If Chou and Chin and Han had
Been dynasties sans *manhood*
And never warred on Mongols at each juncture,
Ah, then I would dare say 't all
You wouldn't have the Great Wall
No noodles, guns—alas, no acupuncture!

The will! The will! The will to go and fight!
The will! The will—to set the world aright!

ROOSEVELT: *(handing a sheaf of papers to Brumby)* I want these messages dispatched with the highest priority.

BRUMBY: Yes, sir.

ROOSEVELT: *(with a naughty grin)* Have you any idea what those messages might be, Mr. Brumby?

BRUMBY: I'm not sure, sir, but may I hazard a guess?

ROOSEVELT: You may.

BRUMBY: *(smiling mischievously)* Have they, perhaps, something to do with the will to war?

ROOSEVELT: Bully, Mr. Brumby! The first is my instruction to the European and South Atlantic Squadron on where to rendezvous if war breaks out. The second . . . *(he stops as* BRUMBY *begins to look worried).* What's the matter, Mr. Brumby? Something bothering you?

BRUMBY: Nothing, sir, really, except that er . . . I just thought . . .

ROOSEVELT: Thought what, Mr. Brumby?

BRUMBY: Begging your pardon, sir, I sort of thought Secretary Long might . . . uh wish to issue that first order himself, sir. It does sound so terribly of the highest level . . .

ROOSEVELT: Mr. Brumby, you're an idiot! I thought we had just agreed on the need to give this country the will to fight.

BRUMBY: Yes, sir, but . . .

ROOSEVELT: But what, Mr. Brumby? Would you give up these precious few hours which God and Mr. Long have given us to put history on its proper course? Bah! Go and see that those messages are sent now!

BRUMBY: *(somewhat penitent)* Aye, aye, sir *(he hurries out left).*

LODGE: *(eagerly)* Theodore!

ROOSEVELT: Yes?

LODGE: The instructions . . . the rest of the instructions . . . .

ROOSEVELT: Aha, Cabot . . . Of course . . . .

(Sings and recites. Arrangement is a la John Philip Sousa; drums outstanding.)

> *I have instructed all the squadrons*
> *in Europe and the Atlantic*
> *On where they must rendezvous!*

LODGE: If war breaks out!

ROOSEVELT:
> *I've told each fleet commander:*
> *"Be cool, Do not be frantic*
> *And fill your ships with coal anew!"*

LODGE: Prepare to bout!

ROOSEVELT:
> *I have purchased all the coal up–*
> *that indispensable mineral*
> *on sale in the Far East–and then*

LODGE: Go buy some more!

ROOSEVELT:
> *I've written confidentially*
> *to the New York Adjutant-General*
> *To be prepared to give us men*

LODGE: In case of war!

ROOSEVELT:
> *I've ordered cannon transferred*
> *to our New York station*
> *And countless ammunition rounds.*

LODGE: Boom! Boom! Boom!

ROOSEVELT:
I've even written Congress
for speedy legislation
Enlisting seamen without bounds.

LODGE: Spanish doom!

(*ROOSEVELT and* LODGE *do a marching dance around the room for a few seconds.*)

LODGE: (*panting a little*) Theodore, there are two or three other Americans I would have liked to have with us at this momentous hour. Alfred Thayer Mahan, Admiral, the designer of our blueprint for empire, the believer in the power of the sea.

ROOSEVELT: Albert J. Beveridge, soon to be Senator from Indiana, one of the most articulate proponents of American expansion, who understands that trade must go with production.

LODGE: And the Reverend Josiah Strong, who knows that the world can be evangelized only by the Anglo-Saxon race.

ROOSEVELT: Yes, what nobler forums for empire than the classrooms of the Naval War College, the Senate, *and* the Congregational Church of Cincinnati! Pity we can't have them with us.

NARRATOR: But they're here, gentlemen. The theatre allows us their presence.

(*Spot on* REV. JOSIAH STRONG, *on different stage level, delivering a lecture at the Congregational Church in Cincinnati, Ohio*)

STRONG: Every race which has deeply impressed itself on the human family has been the representative of some great idea—one or more—which has given direction to the nation's life and form to its civilization.

(Spot on MAHAN, *before a class at the Naval War College)*

MAHAN: Indications are not wanting of an approaching change in the thoughts and policy of the Americans as to their relations in the world outside their borders. The interesting and significant feature of this changing attitude is the turning of eyes outward, instead of inward only, to seek the welfare of the country.

(Spot on BEVERIDGE, *addressing the Middlesex Club of Massachusetts)*

BEVERIDGE: American factories are making more than the American people can use; American soil is producing more than they can consume. Fate has written our policy for us; we must get an ever increasing portion of foreign trade.

STRONG: Among the Egyptians this seminal idea was life, among the Persians it was light, among the Hebrews it was purity, among the Greeks it was beauty, among the Romans it was law. No Biblical reality is of a deeper meaning than that now, America is, indeed, her brother's keeper.

BEVERIDGE: We shall establish trading posts throughout the world as distributing points for American products. We shall cover the oceans with our merchant marine. We shall build a navy to the measure of greatness.

NARRATOR: But sir, hasn't there been a looking outward of Americans for more than a century now?
After all, wasn't there a merchant ship, the *Empress
of China,* I remember reading, which sailed from
New York to Canton five years before the inaugura-
tion of George Washington?

MAHAN: You're quite right, sir. We have been looking
outward for over a century, but we have never had
the power, the sea power, sir, to make that look
really meaningful and profitable. It is true, sir, we
have had our early pioneers, out westward movement. As early as 1776, the American Marco Polo,
Ledyard of Connecticut, sailed away with Captain
Cook around the Cape. He was the first to stir up
American hysteria with prospects of the Orient.

ROOSEVELT: The West had to be taken to reach the East
by ship, so Jefferson sent Lewis and Clark to explore
territory west of the Mississippi River, on and on
from dawn till dark.

MAHAN: Then we swore to rid the west of Spaniards, of
Frenchmen, and the British, Russian, and Mexican.

BEVERIDGE: We bought Louisiana and just to make
things skittish—

LODGE: We drew the line at Oregon

NARRATOR: With "Fifty-Four

MAHAN: Forty—or Fight!"

ROOSEVELT: Then downward to California, Texas.
When the dollar could not buy a piece of land—

BEVERIDGE: We sent our men to live there and then to
cry, "Annex us!"

MAHAN: And that is how they all lie at our command!

ROOSEVELT: And now we're face to face with that ocean called Pacific. Shall its waters take us to—

STRONG: Our destiny?

BEVERIDGE: Great colonies, flying our flag and trading with us, will grow about our posts of trade. Our institutions will follow our flag on the wings of commerce.

ROOSEVELT: Yes, if we can make our shipping yards prolific and build a thousand dreadnought new for our navy.

STRONG: The God of civilization has willed it! *(sings solemnly, like a hymn)*

And now we come to those ideas of the Anglo-Saxon
Those two which led our race relentlessly to wax on:

Namely, civil liberty that gives men true equality
And Christianity less Romanish frivolity!

These are the dual forces that push civilizations.
They are exclusive attributes of Anglo-Saxon nations.
The most efficient teachers of these concepts esoteric are
Of course the Anglo-Saxons who live in North America!

This in fact's the scientific and astute opinion
Of him who authored all those brilliant theories Darwinian
We are the perfect products of a natural selection.
In our veins superior traits have entered by injection!

Let there be no more waiting, no further inhibition,
To conquer and to educate is our Divine Commission;
No Biblical reality is of a meaning deeper
Than that America is now, indeed, her brother's keeper!

A-men!

CONGREGATION: *(off stage)* A-men!

(Four more spotlights now reveal on various stage levels ROOSEVELT, LODGE, MAHAN, *and* BEVERIDGE *with their heads bowed in reverence as* STRONG *repeats his last two lines. They join together with off stage chorus.)*

(*harmonizing*)

No Biblical reality is of a meaning deeper
Than that America is now, her brother's keeper!

A-men! A-men!

ROOSEVELT: Peace may be victory to Bryan and to Hoar

LODGE: There is no peace more permanent than what is won in war!

BEVERIDGE: What should be the policy of this war? Cuba must fall into our hands, but that will be only when Spain is conquered. Our warships today surround Cuba; our armies are massing for Cuba. And yet Cuba will be the last to fall. In the Pacific is the true field of our earliest operations. There Spain has an island empire, the Philippine archipelago. It is poorly defended. Spain's best ships are on the Atlantic side. In the Pacific the United States has a powerful squadron. The Philippines are logically our first target.

(There is a grand and sudden musical flourish after the word "target." The spotlights go out abruptly on all except ROOSEVELT *and* LODGE. *Lights are now full on stage revealing Roosevelt's office.)*

ROOSEVELT: The Philippines are logically our first target. Bravo, Beveridge! *(buzzes Brumby)* Take this down, Brumby. Urgent. Commodore George E.

Dewey. *U.S.S. Olympia.* Asiatic Squadron. Order the squadron except *Monocacy* to Hong Kong. Keep full of coal. In the event of declaration of war with Spain, your duty will be to see that the Spanish squadron does not leave the Asiatic coast and then *(he pauses and winks at Lodge)* offensive operations in Philippine Islands. Signed. Roosevelt. Acting Secretary.

BRUMBY: *(to himself)* The Philippines *(his face brightens as he remembers)* Emilie! Emilie is there with her father. Sweet little Emilie with the blond pigtails. It's been five years. I wonder what she looks like now.

(Stage darkens. Spotlight is on EMILIE WILLIAMS, *blonde, 21, pert but concerned, in cool tropical dress against the background of the Walled City of Manila.)*

EMILIE: War? War with Spain? Father says it is coming. Our navy is coming? To do what? To sink the Spanish fleet. Will they help these people set themselves free? *(changes to girlish expression)* The navy! Who do I know in the navy? Let's see. There's Bill Browning. Freckles. Ted Moore. Buckteeth. And Tom! Tom Brumby. But I hear he's in Washington. It would be nice to see someone like him sailing into Manila Bay—to help to free these people—and *(giggles)* to see me.

(Stage darkens. Full lights again revealing Roosevelt's office.)

BRUMBY: Destiny—and—who knows—Emilie too! *(with decision)* Mr. Secretary . . .

ROOSEVELT: Yes, my dear Mr. Brumby?

BRUMBY: I know this is highly irregular, sir, but . . . but . . .

ROOSEVELT: *(not impatiently)* Yes, yes ...

BRUMBY: I wonder if you could intercede with Secretary Long for me sir. I ... I would like an assignment with the Asiatic squadron. I'd like to see some of that action. After all, sir, I have been with Mr. Long now for more than two years and *(he pauses and puts on a solemn look)* I want to do my share in the shaping of our destiny.

ROOSEVELT: Say no more, Mr. Brumby! God bless you! Go and get the orders ready and I'll sign them. Hurry or you might get there just in time to salvage the Spanish ships in Manila Bay!

BRUMBY: Aye, aye, sir. Thank you, sir!

(He exits excitedly. ROOSEVELT *and* LODGE *slap each other's back in glee.)*

ROOSEVELT: Ho-ho Cabot! It's done! By gad, it's done!

LODGE: *(suddenly worried)* Do you think Dewey can do it? Is he really capable?

ROOSEVELT: I handpicked Dewey myself. Confidentially I had to go over Long's head to do it. Dewey is a good man, Cabot. He served with Farragut in the Civil War. He is as aggressive as Farragut. And what's more, Cabot *(smiling cunningly and nudging* LODGE *playfully),* he is as convinced as we are that war with Spain is inevitable!

LODGE: Then it *is* done. Destiny is on its way.

ROOSEVELT: *(with sincere feeling)* Manifest destiny, Cabot. Manifest destiny.

BLACK OUT

Act One, Scene 2

NARRATOR: "The Mansion," a public house on River Valley Road in a suburb of Singapore. Time: 9:00 P.M., April 22, 1898. GENERAL EMILIO AGUINALDO, exiled leader of Philippine Revolutionary forces, has accepted an invitation to a meeting by U.S. CONSUL GENERAL E. SPENCER PRATT. They are seated around a table in a dimly lit room with HOWARD W. BRAY, an Englishman who once resided in the Philippines and who acts as interpreter, and COL. GREGORIO DEL PILAR, Aguinaldo's aide.

PRATT: General Aguinaldo, I need not stress how full of admiration we Americans are for you and your revolutionaries. But . . .

BRAY: *(stopping PRATT as if to indicate he prefers to translate in short sentences; he speaks Spanish with an English accent)* El Señor Consul desea informarle cuanto les admiran los norteamericanos a usted y a sus compañeros en la revolución.

AGUINALDO: El Señor Consul es muy amable.

PRATT: But I cannot help wonder why you agreed to the Pact of Biak-na-Bato.

BRAY: Mr. Pratt, I lived in the Philippines for fifteen years and I think I can explain . . .

PRATT: *(cutting Bray short)* I'd rather hear the General's own views if you don't mind, Mr. Bray.

BRAY: Eer . . . harrumph . . . of course. El Señor Consul desea saber porqué llegaron ustedes a firmar el Pacto de Biak-na-Bato.

AGUINALDO: Los españoles pidieron la paz. Prometieron reformas, la representación de las Filipinas en los Cortes, la libertad de la palabra y de la prensa, y la expulsión de los frailes mequetrefes.

(BRAY *makes a move to translate but he continues.*)

Aceptamos una indemnización de cuatro cientos mil dolares y nos conformamos, yo y diezinueve de mis oficiales, a exilarnos voluntariamente.

BRAY: The Spaniards sued for peace. They promised reforms, Philippine representation in the Cortes, freedom of speech and the press and the expulsion of meddlesome friars. In exchange, we accepted an indemnity of $400,000 and I and nineteen of my ranking officers agreed to voluntary exile.

PRATT: And have the Spaniards lived up to any of their promises?

BRAY: Y acaso los espanoles . . .

AGUINALDO: (*indicating he has understood the question*) No, no han cumplido ni una promesa.

PRATT: (*standing up with a note of triumph*) That's the crux of the situation, General. As long as the Spaniards have failed to fulfill their bargain, you have the right to resume the revolution!

BRAY: ¡Ya que los españoles no han cumplido sus promesas, tenéis el derecho de resumir la revolución!

AGUINALDO: (*enthusiastically*) ¡Claro que sí!

PRATT: (*pursuing triumphal note*) General, as of the other day, April 19th, Spain and America have been at

war. Now is the time for you to strike. Ally your-
selves with America and you will surely defeat the
Spaniards!

BRAY: América y España han estado en guerra desde el
19 de este. Esta es la hora. ¡Aliaros con América y
venceréis a los espanoles!

(AGUINALDO *is momentarily speechless. He exchanges glances
with his aide.*)

AGUINALDO: (*to* DEL PILAR) ¿Ano Kaya? ¿Mapagka-
katiwalaan kaya natin ang mga ito?

PRATT: America will help you if you will help America!

BRAY: ¡América les ayudará si ustedes ayudan a
América!

AGUINALDO: (*slowly recovering from obvious pleasant shock*)
¿Qué ganamos ayudando a América?

BRAY: What can we expect to gain by helping America?

PRATT: (*quickly*) America will give you much greater
liberty and much more material benefits than the
Spaniards ever promised you.

BRAY: América les dará mayor libertad y mucho más
beneficios materiales que los que les han prometido
los españoles.

(AGUINALDO *turns and exchanges whispers with* DEL PILAR.)

DEL PILAR: Pilitin ninyong sumulat sila ng isang
katibayan.

AGUINALDO: Si no les importa, nos convendría más
poner todo por escrito.

BRAY: If you don't mind, we would prefer to have everything in writing.

PRATT: You need not worry about America.

BRAY: No hay nada que dudar de América.

AGUINALDO: Si, pero . . .

PRATT: The American Congress and President have just made a solemn declaration disclaiming any desire to possess Cuba and promising to leave the country to the Cubans after having driven away the Spaniards and pacified the country.

BRAY: El Congreso americano y el Presidente . . .

AGUINALDO: *(waiving translation)* Pero Cuba no es Filipinas.

PRATT: But that's just it. As in Cuba so in the Philippines. Even more so. After all, Cuba is at our door while the Philippines is ten thousand miles away!

AGUINALDO: (PRATT *has made himself understood by his gesticulations and* AGUINALDO *springs excitedly to his feet. He paces the room for a few moments and then turns slowly to* BRAY.) ¿Pero qué dice Dewey?

PRATT: I have already communicated with him and he says that the United States will recognize the independence of the Philippines under the protection of the United States Navy.

BRAY: Dewey ya ha prometido que los Estado Unidos reconocerán la independencia de Filipinas bajo la protección de su marina.

AGUINALDO: *(nodding with restrained pleasure)* Entonces entremos en un acuerdo por escrito.

BRAY: Then let's have a written agreement.

PRATT: *(half pleading, half impatient)* General, there is no need of a written agreement. The word of the Commodore and *(somewhat pompously)* of the American Consul General to Singapore is equivalent to the most solemn pledge.

BRAY: No hay necesidad de convenios por escrito. La palabra del comodoro y del Consul General Norteamericano a Singapore es equivalente a la mas solemne promesa.

PRATT: *(already orating)* Our verbal assurances will be honored to the letter and should not be classed *(indignantly)* with Spanish promises or Spanish notions of honor *(solemnly raising his forefinger)* The Government of the United States is a very honest, just, and powerful government!

(AGUINALDO *has understood and is ready to believe and accede. He puts on a somewhat naive smile, moves towards* PRATT *and offers him his hand.*)

AGUINALDO: *(brokenly)* I ... trust ... you. Vamos a ayudar a América. Si obtenemos armas, le prometo que nuestro pueblo una vez mas se alzará unido contra los españoles.

BRAY: *(slapping* PRATT *on the back, slightly annoying him)* They will help! They will help! Congratulations my dear consul! Give them the arms and the Filipinos will rise once more against Spain!

PRATT: *(shaking* AGUINALDO's *hand, embracing him, remaining composed but barely hiding conspiratory satisfaction)* Gracias. Gracias, general. You should now leave Singapore at once and rendezvous with Commodore Dewey at Mirs Bay near Hong Kong. And then—on to Manila!

(The four have taken hold of their glasses and now drink a toast)

ALL: On to Manila!

BLACKOUT

Act One, Scene 3

NARRATOR: Hong Kong. Evening of April 26, 1898. At a party given by a British Regiment in honor of Commodore George R. Dewey and his officers. LT. BRUMBY has just arrived in Hong Kong to join the Asiatic Squadron under orders personally signed by Acting Secretary of the Navy Theodore Roosevelt.

BRUMBY: Yes, sir. I arrived from Washington only two weeks ago and joined the squadron at Nagasaki.

BRITISH OFFICER 1:   I hear you were aide to your First Lord of the Admirality.

BRUMBY: *(a bit annoyed with the terminology)* To the Secretary of the Navy, sir.

B/O 1:   *(condescendingly)* Of course.

BRUMBY: I asked to be transferred to sea duty when I saw war coming with Spain.

BRITISH OFFICER 2:   I must say that that was dashed sporting of you.

BRUMBY: I couldn't miss the chance sir. America is flexing her muscles and I want to be in on it.

B/O 1:   It's really more than just a flexing of muscles, isn't it? *(with a rather superior air)* Looks more to me like you were getting ready to whip up an empire of your own, eh leftenant?

BRUMBY: Well, we look on it as more than just empire-building, sir. Rather more like "taking up the white man's burden," as your own countryman would put it.

B/O 2:   Our countryman?

BRUMBY: Ever hear of Rudyard Kipling?

B/O 2:   Ever hear of Kip—! Don't be absurd, sir. Kipling's standard reading at officers' quarters, of course. But I don't recall anything on "the white man's burden."

BRUMBY: He's written a new poem with exactly that exciting title: "The White Man's Burden." But it's still unpublished. He sent Mr. Theodore Roosevelt an advance copy and I overheard Mr. Roosevelt telling Senator Lodge that he thought it was bad poetry but good for expansionism. *I* think it's great!

B/O 1:   What's it about?

BRUMBY: About the Americans going to the Philippines.

B/O 1:   Oh?

BRUMBY: Yes (*recites, trying to remember Kipling's lines*).

Take up the white man's burden
Send forth the best ye breed.
Go bind your sons to exile
To serve your captives need

(sings and recites in waltz time)

Take up the white man's burden
That is the call that we
Lately have overheard in
Shaping our destiny.

B/O 1:

Yes, take up Britannia's burden,
She's lost her appetite;
It's time that she deferred in
Favor of Yankee might!

BOTH:

When we're in our barracks
and tippling;
We go in hysterics
On Kipling!

Take up the white man's burden
That is what Kipling writes;
Kipling has never erred in
Matters concerning whites!

(*The British and American officers now execute a dance in waltz time symbolic of taking up the white man's burden.* BRUMBY *and* B/O 1 *duet while the others dance.*)

BRUMBY: B/O 1:

Take up   *Might is right—*
    the white man's burden   *if you're white!*
That is the call that we   *Do not ask! Do the task!*

Lately have overheard in
Shaping our destiny!

Be resigned! It's divined!
It is your destiny!

We'll take up
    Britannia's burden
She lost her appetite;
It's time that she deferred in
Favor of Yankee might!

We can't last,
    at this blast!
We are très fatigué!
See our grief! Give relief!
Give us your Yankee might!

BOTH:

When we're in our barracks
And tippling
We go in hysterics
On Kipling!

BRUMBY:

Take up
    the white man's burden
That is what Kipling writes
Kipling has never erred in
Matters concerning whites!

B/O 1:

I say theah,
    obey theah!
It is written by a Briton!
I'm tinglish! He's English!
He knows abouts us whites!

BRUMBY:

We must have eased your burden
When we declared our kicks
Versus King George the Third in
Seventeen Seventy Six!

B/O 1:

You did not ease our burden
When you resolved to fight—
That is not Kipling's wording
You, sir, are also white!

BOTH:

> *When your fellow white*
> *You're crippling,*
> *That does not excite*
> *R. Kipling!*
>
> *For here's the white man's burden:*
> *Civilize all in sight*
> *Specially those befurred in*
> *Skins that are not so light!*

NARRATOR: The guest of honor, COMMODORE GEORGE DEWEY. With him are ROUNCEVILLE WILDMAN, the American Consul to Hong Kong, and OSCAR F. WILLIAMS, the American Consul to Manila, who has been summoned to Hong Kong by Dewey.

DEWEY: Consul Williams, I trust you had a good crossing from Manila.

WILLIAMS: It's usually rough just outside Manila Bay. But one does recover fast enough, thank you, Commodore.

DEWEY: Fine. I sent for you because I'd like your personal view of the situation in Manila.

WILLIAMS: Well, sir, I would say conditions in the Philippines and Cuba would be practically alike. There is a war, sir, and battles are almost a daily occurence. The insurgents are being armed and drilled and are rapidly increasing.

DEWEY: *(a little impatiently)* Yes, yes. I've read your report on that. I'm really interested in the disposition of Spanish forces.

WILLIAMS: The Boca Grande channel is mined, sir—the one, I presume, you had expected to use for your squadron's entry into Manila Bay.

DEWEY: Oh? (*apparently not disturbed*) Yes, that confirms Consul Pratt's cable from Singapore. He got it from a steamer which arrived there from Manila the other day.

WILDMAN: Does this upset your plans, sir?

DEWEY: Not really, Mr. Wildman. Laying mines is not an easy thing. I recall the alleged mining of the Suez Canal during the Arabi Pasha rebellion. An Italian torpedo expert didn't take it seriously and steamed harmlessly through the canal. I don't think the Spaniards will be any better than the Egyptians at laying a mine blockade.

WILLIAMS: Well, in fact, sir, you may not have to run the blockade to fight the Spaniards.

DEWEY: What do you mean?

WILLIAMS: Just as I was leaving Manila I got an unconfirmed report that the Spanish squadron was sailing out of Manila Bay into Subic Bay.

DEWEY: What?

WILDMAN: Is that bad, sir?

DEWEY: Of course it's bad, Mr. Wildman. Hmmm. Admiral Montojo seems to have realized the strategic advantage of Subic over Manila at the last moment. We'll have to alter our battle plans.

WILLIAMS: I'm sorry about that, sir. Ah, one more thing, Commodore . . .

DEWEY: Yes.

WILLIAMS: About the Filipinos . . .

DEWEY: What about them?

WILLIAMS: Well, sir, there's talk of their organizing a republic and they're counting on our support.

DEWEY: I hope you haven't made them any promises.

WILLIAMS: Oh no, sir. But I thought that if we are liberating the Cubans we might do the same for the Filipinos.

WILDMAN: I would like to say "Amen" to that, Commodore.

DEWEY: *(Caesar-like)* You too, Wildman?

WILDMAN: *(not with too much confidence)* Yes, sir. I've been talking to Don Felipe Agoncillo, the revolutionary junta's representative on foreign relations, a most cultured gentleman. He has proposed an immediate and automatic alliance. He offered to buy 20,000 Springfield rifles and *(he puts on a slightly avaricious look)* is willing to allow the United States 25 to 30 percent profit!

DEWEY: Great Godfrey, Mr. Wildman, you didn't make *him* any promises, did you?

WILDMAN: *(retreating)* Oh no, sir. I'm still waiting for the State Department's approval.

DEWEY   Good! You'll never get it!

WILDMAN: *(cautiously)* But I understand Consul Pratt in Singapore has already . . .

DEWEY: Oh, yes, that Pratt. I hear he's been receiving Filipino serenaders from his balcony at the Raffles Hotel!

WILDMAN: He's done more than that, sir. I understand he has informed General Aguinaldo that you have said that the United States will recognize the independence of the Philippines under the protection of the United States Navy!

DEWEY: I have said no such thing!

WILDMAN: Aguinaldo is coming to Hong Kong to join you, sir.

DEWEY: I know he is. I authorized Pratt to tell him he could come. I thought he might have valuable information we could use.

WILLIAMS: *(timidly reentering conversation)* Begging your pardon, sir. May I venture to suggest that you might find General Aguinaldo ready to give you something a bit more valuable than information?

DEWEY: Of course. Our purpose is to weaken the Spaniards in every way. We want a quick end to this war to free Cuba from Spanish oppression. Under certain restrictions, we would welcome operations by the insurgents against Spanish oppression in the Philippines.

(WILDMAN *and* WILLIAMS *beam happily*)

DEWEY: But I cannot promise to support Philippine independence!

(WILDMAN'S *and* WILLIAM'S *faces drop*)

Gentlemen, you might as well know this. Secretary Long has sent me a cable on this matter. I remember his exact words. I am "not to have political alliances with the insurgents or any faction in the islands that would incur liability to maintain their cause in the future."

(WILDMAN *and* WILLIAMS *look at each other in silence*)

By the way, why isn't Aguinaldo here yet?

WILDMAN: He's coming on the British steamer *Malacca* which should be docking tomorrow morning.

DEWEY: Well, we sail tomorrow afternoon. If he's not here by then, we'll sail without him.

WILDMAN: Yes, sir.

(WILDMAN *and* WILLIAMS *walk to backstage.* DEWEY *remains in front. Lights dim. Waltz music changes as* DEWEY *sings with spotlight on him.*)

DEWEY: These tiresome consuls! If they had their way . . . (*sings*)

Williams, Wildman, and Pratt!
Our destiny and all of that
Would on its face fall flat
If they had their own way!

Williams, Wildman, and Pratt!
They'd like to play the Democrat
And never teach the little brown brat
The American way!

I did not work my head off
To gain this choice command—

Just to win in the water
And then give up the land!

Williams, Wildman, and Pratt!
Each one a meddling diplomat
Who'd make fight a useless
battle in Manila Bay!

(DEWEY goes into a soft shoe. He resumes singing.)

I will not sail to bring down
Castilian tyranny,
Just to give the Tagalog
His independency!

Williams, Wildman, and Pratt!
I'd never get an Admiral's hat
Nor on the New York Herald mat
If they had their own way!

(A BRITISH OFFICER *approaches* DEWEY)

DEWEY: Brumby! (BRUMBY *approaches from one side, as*
WILLIAMS *and his daughter* EMILIE *approach from the*
other.)

WILLIAMS: Commodore, may I present my daughter,
Emilie. Commodore George Dewey.

BRUMBY: Emilie?

EMILIE: Tom?

DEWEY and WILLIAMS: Oh! You know each other?

BRUMBY and EMILIE: Er . . .

DEWEY: Come along, Mr. Williams, we have business.
(exit)

WILLIAMS: We do? Oh, yes, yes, of course. *(exit)*

BRUMBY: Emilie. It's really you. You are even lovelier than I imagined when I volunteered to come.

EMILIE: And you—you look fine in that uniform, Tom. But I thought you were in Washington.

BRUMBY: And I thought you were in Manila. I was looking forward to seeing you there. Your father is still consul there, isn't he?

EMILIE: Yes. He brought me here to keep me safe until you sink the Spanish fleet in Manila Bay.

BRUMBY: That shouldn't take too long. You'll be back in Manila in a few days, when the whole place is under the American flag.

EMILIE: What about the flag of the Filipinos?

BRUMBY: What about it?

EMILIE: After all, it is still their country, you know.

BRUMBY: I don't know about them. I know about our destiny. I volunteered to serve Commodore Dewey to complete it *(eager to change the subject)* and to see you again. And that means it is now *our* destiny —yours *(brashly)* and mine!

EMILIE: *(coyly)* Indeed, Lt. Brumby?

BRUMBY: *(in feigned formality)* Indeed, Miss Williams. As Mr. Kipling says, it's the white man's burden. And you make a lovely white partner to share it with. Emilie, Emilie, Emilie . . .

(Sings. Tune is as in "White Man's Burden.")

It won't be such a burden
To reach our destiny,
Now that my heart is spurred in
Pursuit of Emilie!

EMILIE:

It will be quite a burden
For you to reach poor me,
I have not yet concurred in
Your view of destiny!

My heartbeat may now
be tripling;
Yet, I cannot bow
to Kipling!

BRUMBY:

You will accept that burden,
My dearest Emilie,
For it will now be shared in
Lightly by you and me!

BRUMBY:
It won't be such a burden
To reach
     our destiny,
Now that my heart is spurred in
Pursuit of Emilie!

EMILIE:
It will be quite a burden
For you to catch poor me,
I have not yet concurred in
Your view of destiny!

EMILIE:
Do not rush! I may blush!
This is wrong—
     in Hong Kong
Don't race heah–in Asia!
Poor little Emilie!

BRUMBY:
No, not quite, 'twill be light!
Not at all! You will fall!
In due time–we will rhyme
Singing of destiny!

BOTH:
Our heartbeats may now
Be tripling!

EMILIE:
Yet, I cannot bow
To Kipling!

BRUMBY:
You will accept that burden
My dearest Emilie,
For it will now be shared in
Lightly by you and me!

EMILIE:
But I choose to refuse!
This is too impromptu
I don't care—I won't share!
That kind of destiny!

EMILIE:
But I choose to refuse!
I won't share that kind of destiny!

BLACKOUT

Act One, Scene 4

NARRATOR: The forward deck of the *U.S.S. Olympia.*
Time: Just before dawn, May 1, 1898. JOSEPH L.
STICKNEY, an Annapolis graduate, now a corre-
spondent for the *New York Herald,* is reading his
report of the Battle of Manila Bay. Already on the
bridge are some of Commodore Dewey's staff:
COMMANDER B.P. LAMBERTON, Chief of Staff;
LIEUTENANT C.P. REES, Executive Officer;
LIEUTENANT T.F. BRUMBY, Flag Lieutenant;
LIEUTENANT C.G. CALKINS, navigator, and an old
seaman, PURDY, a privileged character because he
has served in the Navy for over forty years.

NARRATOR/STICKNEY: *(reading aloud)* When we arrived at the entrance to Subic Bay early in the afternoon, the *Boston,* the *Baltimore* and the *Concord,* which had been sent in to reconnoitre it, came out of the Bay and reported that the Spaniards had neither ships nor shore guns in the harbor. Our course for Manila was resumed. The final preparations for battle have been made. At the moment, Commodore Dewey is in war council with all the commanding officers of the squadron which is composed of the flagship *Olympia,* the *Baltimore,* the *Petrel,* the *Boston,* the *Raleigh,* and the *Concord.* The Spanish squadron is composed of the flagship *Reina Castilla,* the *Isla de Cuba,* the *Don Juan de Austria,* the *Isla de Luzon,* the *Marqués del Duero,* and the *Don Antonio de Ulloa.*

(COMMODORE DEWEY *enters left wearing a white uniform but with a gray traveling cap. He is accompanied by* CAPT. C.V. GRIDLEY, *the commanding officer of the* Olympia.)

NARRATOR/STICKNEY: *(standing up)* Good morning, Commodore.

DEWEY: Good morning *(recognizing Stickney in the semi-darkness).* Oh yes, Stickney. I've been meaning to send for you. You're an Annapolis graduate, aren't you?

NARRATOR/STICKNEY: Yes, sir. I served in the Navy a few years before resigning to join the *New York Herald,* sir. You see, sir I . . .

DEWEY: I understand, Mr. Stickney. There's no need to explain. Without battle, navy life can be tedious, eh? In any case, how would you like to return to the service?

NARRATOR/STICKNEY: Sir?

DEWEY: Ensign Caldwell, my flag secretary, has very gallantly volunteered for duty at the guns and I have decided to appoint you my aide. You will take station with me at the forward bridge.

NARRATOR/STICKNEY: *(excitedly dropping pencil and pad)* Yes, sir!

DEWEY: *(winking one eye)* Satisfied?

NARRATOR/STICKNEY: Yes, sir! Thank you, sir! Aye, aye, sir!

DEWEY: Then come on *(he starts to climb to bridge but notices* PURDY, *who is pretending to sweep the deck at an obviously ungodly hour).* Well, Purdy, what is it?

PURDY: *(saluting)* I hope, sir, that ye don't intend to keep the fight up until the 3rd of May.

DEWEY: And why not? *(looks aside in mock indignation at* STICKNEY *who has been taking notes)*

PURDY: You see, sir, I got licked the last time I fought on the 3rd of May.

DEWEY: *(now thoroughly amused but kindly)* Oh? And where was that?

PURDY: At Chancellorsville, sir. My boxing name was "Fighting Joe" Hooker, sir.

DEWEY: *(laughing heartily in spite of himself)* All right, Purdy. I promise you it won't last till the 3rd. We'll fight only today and you'll have another kind of May Anniversary to think about. Remember that, my man.

(DEWEY, GRIDLEY, *and* STICKNEY *proceed to the bridge where they take positions.*)

DEWEY: Gridley . . .

GRIDLEY: Sir?

DEWEY: I see no sense in risking the loss of all our senior officers by one shell. Perhaps it would be best if you stationed yourself at the conning tower.

GRIDLEY: Aye, aye, sir *(he ascends to conning tower).*

NARRATOR/STICKNEY: *(who has been staring at Dewey's cap)* Begging your pardon, sir.

DEWEY: Yes, Stickney?

NARRATOR/STICKNEY: Is that traveling cap a kind of good luck charm?

DEWEY: Eh? *(he removes cap and looks at it)* Oh! of course not, Stickney. I couldn't find my service cap after the guns in my cabin had been cleared for action *(as* STICKNEY *takes note he scans horizon with binoculars).* We ought to have a shot from Corregidor very soon now. You may take her up to eight knots, Calkins. We shouldn't do more than that or we'll leave our supply ships too far behind.

VOICE OFFSTAGE: Aye, aye, sir.

NARRATOR/STICKNEY: *(reading)* A shell screamed over our ship, followed by another. There was no panic on the bridge.

VOICE OFFSTAGE: It's the Corregidor batteries, sir.

NARRATOR/STICKNEY: There was firing from the other ships of the squadron. After a few volleys, there was complete silence. Dewey, cooly unimpressed, was looking through his binoculars.

VOICE OFFSTAGE: Manila in sight, sir.

DEWEY: *(showing slight reaction)* Bring her down to four knots, Calkins.

VOICE OFFSTAGE: Aye, aye, sir.

NARRATOR/STICKNEY: Dewey continued looking through his binoculars. Shells began to burst all around. It was now daybreak.

VOICE OFFSTAGE: It's the Manila batteries, sir. The *Concord* and the *Boston* are replying.

DEWEY: Signal them to cease firing. They may cause damage to the city population.

NARRATOR/STICKNEY: Suddenly two great jets of water rose high in the air beside our ship.

VOICE OFFSTAGE: Submarine mines of Cavite, sir. No damage, sir.

NARRATOR/STICKNEY: Dewey remained unconcerned and the rest of the staff looked anxiously at him and at each other. They were itching to hear the order to fire.

DEWEY: *(still at his binoculars)* There's the *Reina Cristina,* the *Castilla,* and the rest of them. Head toward them, Calkins.

VOICE OFFSTAGE: Aye, aye, sir!

NARRATOR/STICKNEY: Shells began to burst all around us, and those at the bridge and the crew below were all looking tensely at Dewey waiting for the order to fire. Dewey was watching the enemy's hot fire as if he were a disinterested spectator of an unusual display of fireworks!

DEWEY: Take her close along the 5-fathom line, Calkins.

VOICE OFFSTAGE: Aye, aye, sir.

DEWEY: But be careful not to get her aground.

NARRATOR/STICKNEY: The firing from the Spanish guns increased and there was again a tense waiting. All eyes were on Dewey. Purdy, who has been bending over, looking eagerly ahead with his hand on the lock of the 5-inch gun, suddenly sprang up and shouted:

PURDY: Boys, remember the *Maine!*

VOICES OFFSTAGE: Remember the *Maine!*

DEWEY: What's the time, Brumby?

BRUMBY: 0540, sir.

NARRATOR/STICKNEY: The shellings from the Spanish squadron continued. Tension showed on all the faces.

DEWEY: *(slowly looking up to* GRIDLEY *in the conning tower, half-shouting but without excitement)* You may fire when you're ready, Gridley.

(The men at the batteries let out a great shout to be drowned out only by their own guns. The noise of battle is deafening. Then the lights dim, the noise is subdued but sustained. The spotlight is on DEWEY.*)*

DEWEY: *(sings)*

> *You may fire when you're ready,*
> *Gridley,*
> *Keep those guns roaring steady,*
> *Gridley,*
> *For the hour of destiny is at hand.*
> *It only waits for your command*
> *to fire!*
> *Inspire*
> *Our sweating men to die!*
> *They know, they know the reason why,*
> *Gridley! Gridley!*

> *You may fire when your're ready, Gridley,*
> *Give 'em one for old Teddy,*
> *Gridley,*
> *Give 'em one for each Republican*
> *Who set the heart of Yankee man*
> *On fire,*
> *On fire,*
> *To aspire,*
> *To see his flag unfurled*
> *Among the tallest in the world,*
> *Gridley, Gridley!*

> *The Anglo-Saxon has always been master*
> *Of that Spanish cannon fodder!*
> *We'll sink Montojo even faster*
> *Than the English sank the Armada!*

> *You may fire when you're ready,*
> *Gridley,*

Let the triumph be heady,
Gridley,
For victory will have this worth:
We'll sweep the darkness from the earth
With fire,
Our fire,
And higher
Will our torches sway
The more you sink in this blasted bay,
Gridley, Gridley, Gridley!
Yes—fire when you're ready,
Gridley,
Let your voice be leady,
Gridley,
Now open up with every gun
And let them bristle in the sun
With fire,
Our fire!
And sire
An empire young and vain
Out of that prostrate woman—Spain,
Gridley, Gridley, Gridley!

(The firing continues but recedes as LAMBERTON *speaks.)*

VOICE OFFSTAGE: Sir, the Spanish flagship *Reina Cristina* is disabled and the Admiral appears to have transferred his flag to the *Isla de Cuba.*

DEWEY: And the rest?

VOICE OFFSTAGE: The *Castilla* is likewise disabled, sir, the *Don Juan de Austria* is badly damaged, the *Isla de Luzon* has three guns dismounted and the *Marqués del Duero* is in a bad way. But the *Don Antonio de Ulloa* still retains her position at Sangley Point.

DEWEY: Hmmm. Signal the squadron to withdraw. It's time for the crew to have breakfast.

BRUMBY: Sir?

DEWEY: Breakfast, Mr. Brumby. The crew only had a cup of coffee at 4 this morning, didn't they?

BLACKOUT

Act One, Scene 5

NARRATOR: Time: June, 1898. Dewey is now a Rear-Admiral.

BRUMBY: And here's Aguinaldo's third proclamation, Admiral.

DEWEY: Read it please, Brumby.

BRUMBY: "The great North American nation, a lover of true liberty, and therefore desirous of liberating our country from the tyranny and despotism to which it has been subjected by its rulers, has decided to give us disinterested protection, considering us able and civilized to govern ourselves (DEWEY *winces*). In order to retain this high opinion of the never to be too highly praised and great nation of North America, we should abominate such acts as pillage and robbery of every description (DEWEY *looks pleased but slightly guilty*). Admiral . . .

DEWEY: Yes?

BRUMBY: This proclamation seems to assume that the United States will recognize the independence of the Filipinos. Does this confirm the rumor that you have given General Aguinaldo this promise?

DEWEY: *(evading the question)* The orders of Secretary Long are that I am, and I quote, not to have political alliances with the insurgents or any faction in the islands that would incur liability to maintain their cause in the future.

BRUMBY: But isn't it amazing how much Aguinaldo has been able to do since you asked him to "go ashore and start your army." He has resumed the revolution—pardon me—insurrection, and in less than two months he has cornered the whole Spanish army inside the Walled City of Manila.

DEWEY: Well, I am waiting for our troops to arrive and the closer Aguinaldo invests the city, the easier it will be when our troops arrive to march in.

BRUMBY: But supposing the Spaniards surrender the city before our troops arrive?

DEWEY: They won't. Those proud Spaniards will never surrender their former colonials. They'd rather surrender to us.

NARRATOR: *(knocks and salutes)* Sir, I have just come from General Aguinaldo.

DEWEY: Well?

NARRATOR: He presents his compliments, sir, and wishes me to inform you that he has issued a Declaration of Independence *(hands declaration to* DEWEY*)*.

He has also proclaimed a revolutionary government and he would like to ask you to be the guest of honor at the inaugural ceremony tomorrow (*hands over written invitation*).

(DEWEY *looks over the declaration and then hands it to* BRUMBY.)

BRUMBY: The revolutionary government is to have a Congress, a Cabinet, a Supreme Court, and so on. This will be a *de facto* government, sir. The Filipinos are losing no time.

DEWEY: (*looking up slowly and pensively from reading the invitation*) Yes, and they can do it. Those people are superior in intelligence and more capable of self-government than the natives of Cuba, and I am familiar with both races.

BRUMBY: (*now somewhat naively assuming that Dewey is accepting the invitation*) Admiral, may I have the honor of accompanying you to the ceremony?

DEWEY: (*as if shaken from reverie*) Eh? Oh! We (*painfully*), we are not going, Brumby.

BRUMBY: (*surprised*) Sir?

DEWEY: I said tell Aguinaldo we're not coming.

BRUMBY: But . . . but . . . should I give a reason, sir?

DEWEY: Reason? (*losing temper*) Why in heaven's name must I give a reason? Tell him—tell him the mail is coming tomorrow and I must be on board when it is distributed!

BRUMBY: *(saluting)* Aye, aye, sir *(casts a puzzled look at* STICKNEY, *who shows a passive face and exits right).*

NARRATOR: *(saluting)* Admiral, we have a signal from the German flagship. Admiral von Diederichs would like to come aboard.

DEWEY: *(exchanging knowing looks with* BRUMBY) Have him come aboard by all means. And get me that report on his men's activities.

BRUMBY: Looks like the old boy has decided to come and pay his respects at last.

DEWEY: I'm not so sure he's coming to pay his respects.

BRUMBY: All the others have—the British, the French, the Japanese. I don't see why he should not.

DEWEY: There are three reasons why he might not, Brumby.

BRUMBY: Namely, sir?

DEWEY: First, unlike the other squadrons, his has more gun-power than ours.

BRUMBY: I didn't know that, sir. Second?

DEWEY: Second, in spite of my promotion to rear-admiral he still outranks me. He's a vice-admiral.

BRUMBY: *(shrugging it off)* And third?

DEWEY: The third is the most important. He's a German! (STICKNEY *joins him in laughter)* But he doesn't bother me. Captain Chichester has assured me of the support of his British ships in case von

Diederichs makes real trouble. Our combined fire-power should be enough answer to the Kaiser.

NARRATOR: VICE-ADMIRAL OTTO VON DIEDERICHS, com-mander of the the German Asiatic Squadron!

(DIEDERICHS *struts in accompanied by three members of his staff.* DEWEY *rises. They exchange salutes.*)

DEWEY: Welcome aboard, Admiral. Gentlemen.

DIEDERICHS: Thank you, Admiral. You will permit me to come to ze point.

DEWEY: Of course.

DIEDERICHS: I have come to demand an apology. Yes-terday your cruiser the *Raleigh* fired a shot across ze bow of our ship ze *Irene*.

DEWEY: Yes, I understand the *Irene* had ignored a de-mand for identification.

DIEDERICHS: By vat right do you demand identification from my ships?

DEWEY: The right of the laws of war, Admiral. We have established a blockade of the port of Manila. Which reminds me—perhaps you'd like to explain your breach of naval etiquette.

DIEDERICHS: Vat breach? Vat etiquette?

DEWEY: You have deployed your ships in Manila Bay without consulting with the commander of the blockading squadron.

DIEDERICHS: I am here by order of ze Kaiser, sir!

DEWEY: Ordered to do what?

DIEDERICHS: To protect ze German interests in Manila!

DEWEY: Lamberton.

LAMBERTON: Sir?

DEWEY: How many German business houses did you say there were in Manila?

LAMBERTON: Only one, sir. A trading firm.

DEWEY: *(while* DIEDERICHS *fumes)* Would you read that report on the activities of the Admiral's men.

LAMBERTON: *(takes report from his pocket and reads)* The officers and men of the German Asiatic Squadron have been engaged in the following activities excess of their rights as a neutral power: 1) They have saluted only the Spanish flag; 2) they have landed sacks of flour for the Spanish and 3) they have entertained Spanish officers and their ladies in their wardrooms; 4) they have taken soundings off the mouth of the Pasig river; 5) they have occupied Mariveles harbor for several days; 6) they have tried to prevent Filipino troops from capturing the Spanish naval post of Grande Island.

DIEDERICHS: *(exploding)* Are you finished?

LAMBERTON: *(a bit flustered)* Er . . . yes, sir.

DIEDERICHS: Vat ve have done is none of your business! Ve have as much right here as you have!

DEWEY: *(himself exploding)* Do you want war?

DIEDERICHS: Certainly not.

DEWEY: Well, it looks like it and you are very near it!

DIEDERICHS: *(throwing up his arms in rage)* Ach! Mein Gott!

DEWEY: As we are in for it now it matters little to us whether we fight Spain or Germany or the world; and if you desire war you can have it right here!

DIEDERICHS: Yah?

DEWEY: Yah! You need not cable to Berlin, nor need I to Washington. You can just have war here and now! (DIEDERICHS *wheels around and is about to leave*) But if you don't want war, then I would suggest . . .

   (Sings. Tune is reprise of first song in Act I.)

   I would suggest, mein Admiral
   that it would be much wiser
   If you returned to Germany
   and told your friend, the Kaiser
   That Dewey and his Yankee ships
   are anchored in Manila
   And he has left no room at all
   for your goddamned flotilla!

DIEDERICHS:

   I have my own suggestion, sir
   millionen donner vetter,
   One vich I think ist gut,
   in fact I think that it ist better.
   Vy don't you take that arrogance
   vich you disguise so thinly
   Und shtick it up the you know vat
   of President McKinley!

DEWEY: You, sir, are insulting our beloved President!

DIEDERICHS: Und to mein lieber Kaiser you are very insolent!

ALL AMERICANS: *(pointing to Germans)* You, sir, are insulting our beloved President!

ALL GERMANS: *(pointing to Americans)* Und to mein lieber Kaiser you are very insolent.

DEWEY:

> *You can not have the Philippines,*
> *I must be quite emphatic.*
> *For we intend to teach them*
> *our traditions democratic.*
> *So I suggest that you get off*
> *and get your fleet in motion*
> *And grab yourselves some other isles*
> *There's plenty in the ocean!*

DIEDERICHS:

> *If I had time I'd go ashore*
> *und show your dirty linen,*
> *Your gott verdamnt hypocrisy*
> *toward den Philippinen!*
> *But I must cable for instructions,*
> *himmel donner blitzen,*
> *This whole affair, mein Admiral,*
> *has got me at vits end!*

DEWEY: You must be resigned, you can not have the Philippines!

DIEDERICHS: Well, in zat case ve sail avay und grab ze Carolines! *(rhymes with "Philippines")*

DEWEY: That's pronounced Carolines, mein Admiral.

DIEDERICHS: So? Vell, in zat case . . . Vy do you not say ve cannot have ze Philippines *(rhymes with "Carolines")*, so therefore I can say zat ve vill grabe ze Carolines?

DEWEY: But I can't, mein Admiral. I am an American. Only the British say Philippines *(rhymes with "Carolines")*.

DIEDERICHS: Ach du lieber . . . Vell zen . . . Vy do you not say ve cannot have den Philippinen, so therefore I can say zat ve vill grab ze Carolinen?.

DEWEY: Oh, all right! *(throws arms up in mock despair)* Oh, all right, you cannot have den blessed Philippinen!

DIEDERICHS: *(relieved)* Ach so! Ve'll say auf wiedersehn und grab ze Carolinen!

ALL AMERICANS: Oh all right, you cannot have den blessed Philippinen!

ALL GERMANS: Ach so! Ve'll say auf wiedersehn und grab ze Carolinen.

ALL ON STAGE:

The will! The will! The will to go and fight!
The will, the will to set the world aright!

BLACKOUT

Act One, Scene 6

NARRATOR: On June 12, 1898, EMILIO AGUINALDO declared the independence of the Philippines in Kawit, Cavite. The Filipinos felt assured of their victory against the Spanish forces because they found in the Americans an ally and a friend. Or so they thought.

BLACKOUT

End of Act One

ACT TWO

Act Two, Scene 1

NARRATOR: Time: August 12, 1898. Fort Santiago in-side the Walled City of Manila, at the mouth of the Pasig River on Manila Bay. FERMIN JAUDENES, Spanish Governor and Captain-General of the Philippines is pacing up and down stage. Sporadic, distant firing is heard in the background. An aide enters.

NARRATOR: Su excelencia, el teniente BRUMBY representando al almirante Dewey y el coronel WHITTIER representando al General Greene.

JAUDENES: Que entren.

(*Enter* LT. BRUMBY *and* COL. WHITTIER. *They salute.* JAUDENES *returns the salute.*)

Gentlemen, pardon my poor English. I consented to accept your presence here—but I will not deal with the natives. That is too much.

WHITTIER: We understand, your excellency.

JAUDENES: Good, I—I hear that your infantry has landed in force.

WHITTIER: You are outnumbered and outgunned,

your excellency. There are almost ten thousand of us ashore and more reenforcements are coming. And there are thousands more of the Filipinos . . .

JAUDENES: *(throwing up his arms)* The Filipinos! There is no such thing! You mean the indios!

WHITTIER: Yes, sir, I mean the indios! They're under control! We have gradually replaced them in the trenches!

JAUDENES: Oh? And why did the indios agree to that?

BRUMBY: Er—in exchange for certain assurances, sir.

JAUDENES: I see.

BRUMBY: You need not surrender to the Fili—I mean—the indios. But would you surrender to us?

JAUDENES: Surrender? *(shocked but accepting reality)* Now? Without a fight?

WHITTIER: A token battle could be arranged.

JAUDENES: A what?

WHITTIER: A token—a sham battle—a . . .

BRUMBY: *(cutting in)* Sir, we could pretend to have a battle.

JAUDENES: *(understanding)* Oh? And how do you suggest this battle?

BRUMBY: Our squadron could exchange sporadic fire with your shore batteries and our soldiers could advance against some firing by yours, and then . . .

JAUDENES: And then we would surrender. And *(sadly)* the honor of Castile is saved.

BRUMBY: *(with sympathy)* Yes, the honor of Castile is saved.

JAUDENES: *(slowly)* So be it.

(Sings. Tune is as in Dewey's song to Gridley but with mournful, Spanish air.)

> *What a way to deceive her, España,*
> *We'll pretend to shout "Viva, España!"*
> *We'll wave our banners gold and red*
> *And fire above the Yankee's head*
> *Again*
> *And again*
> *And then*
> *We'll give up—bowed but brave—*
> *At least her honor we will save,*
> *España, España!*
>
> *They can't say, "Se rindió España"*
> *To the treacherous indio, España!*
> *We'll drink a last Castilian glass*
> *And watch our dying empire pass*
> *Away!*
> *But they*
> *Will say*
> *It died in glorious fight,*
> *At least our conquerors were white!*
> *España, España, España!*

BLACKOUT

Act Two, Scene 2

WILLIAMS: Oh, there you are Tom. I was looking for you because I'd like you to give Admiral Dewey this message.

BRUMBY: Yes, sir.

WILLIAMS: Tell him the Filipinos are getting restless. Aguinaldo rejects any kind of union with the United States. They want us to recognize the Philippines Republic immediately.

BRUMBY: But isn't that just a paper republic, sir?

WILLIAMS: So far, yes. But there is no doubt the Filipinos are determined to make it real. Brumby, do you know that of all the peoples of Asia only the Filipinos have never had a king?

BRUMBY: No. They never really taught us much oriental history in school.

WILLIAMS: Well, it's true. When the Spaniards came four hundred years ago they found independent settlements with their own three-level societies of noblemen, freemen, and serfs—much like the Greek city states. They were called *balagays* and the chief ruled by consent of the freemen.

BRUMBY: But the Spaniards made them forget all that.

WILLIAMS: No, not really, Brumby. They embraced Christianity but never really accepted the Spanish governor and some of the worldly friars. They had a lot of local rebellions for three centuries before they could finally get together in a national revolution.

And that's where we came in. They thought we were coming to help them finish off the Spaniards.

BRUMBY: And we did!

WILLIAMS: Yes, but now they want what they fought for—independence.

BRUMBY: *(unconvinced)* But what kind of an independent government could these people run?

WILLIAMS: They've written a constitution, thirty percent of which consists of a Bill of Rights! I think I have an idea what kind of government they would run. Back home we have a name for it—democracy!

BRUMBY: That's a little hard to believe, sir.

EMILIE: *(who has entered on* BRUMBY's *last line)* What about the Filipinos, Tom? Did they find it hard to believe that our army was coming to liberate them? Why wasn't a single Filipino present at this surrender? This is as much their victory as ours. More! They have been fighting the Spaniards for centuries. And you landed only last month!

BRUMBY: Be realistic, Emilie. The Spaniards would never have surrendered to the Filipinos. It would have meant a long, bloody battle—perhaps thousands of American lives!

EMILIE: If America wanted to save American lives she shouldn't have sent an army here!

BRUMBY: *(slightly exasperated)* Emilie . . .

EMILIE: Tom, this is not the way I saw this at all. Perhaps

I've been naive. Father said Dewey was convinced
that these people deserved their freedom, that our
army was coming to liberate them. How could the
Filipinos accept all this now? Are they as naive as I
am?

BRUMBY: Emilie, America has a destiny to fulfill . . .

EMILIE: At whose expense, Lt. Brumby?

BRUMBY: *(blowing up)* Who cares at whose expense!
(recovering) I mean . . . Oh Emilie . . . I do
care . . . . I mean . . . there are so many more important things to care about. About us, for instance.
I love you, Emilie.

EMILIE: You love me, Tom? What do you know about
love?

BRUMBY: What do you mean?

EMILIE: I mean . . . *(sings)*

Before you can love a woman
You must first be a man

BRUMBY: Man? *(in mocking rage)* why you little squirt!
(advances towards her).

EMILIE:

You must first be a human
And then American . . .

          (BRUMBY retreats, sulking a little)

You must open your eyes,
You must open your eyes,
You musn't be blind!

You must see past your nose
There's a whole world of those
Called humankind!

Men are equal and free,
Men are equal and free,
That's what Jefferson meant!
I was taught this in school
No one ever must rule
Without consent!

If you set other people free
And you don't raise your flag above them,
Then you know what that means to me?
You love them!

Then I'll know that you're fit,
Then I'll know that you're fit
Of love to speak,
Until then understand
You've no right to demand
The love you seek!

BRUMBY: But Emilie . . .

EMILIE:

If you set other people free
And you don't raise your flag above them,
Then you know what that means to me?
You love them!

Then I'll know that you're fit,
Then I'll know that you're fit
Of love to cry . . .
But for now I'm afraid
I have here overstayed
And so—good-bye!

(EMILIE *walks out*)

BRUMBY: Emilie! Wait!

BLACKOUT

Act Two, Scene 3

NARRATOR: Washington, D.C. PRESIDENT WILLIAM MCKINLEY at the White House with a group of visiting Methodist ministers.

MCKINLEY: Gentlemen. When I heard of Dewey's victory in Manila I must confess I could not have told those darned islands within two thousand miles *(the ministers join him in mild laughter)*. The truth is I didn't want the Philippines and when they came to us as a gift from the gods, I did not know what to do with them . . . *(sings)*

Night after night
I paced the floor,
All through the White House
From door to door;
Night after night
From dusk to dawn
I wet my feet on the White House lawn,
Trying to figger what I'druther
Do with that pesky little brown brother,
Trying to figger what I'druther
Do with that pesky little brown brother!

MINISTERS:

> *Pity our President,*
> *Wand'ring in bewilderment*
> *Trying to figger what he'druther*
> *Do with that pesky little brown brother!*

MCKINLEY:

> *I sought in vain*
> *Advice from all,*
> *Even Democrats*
> *At the Capitol;*
> *I thought we'd take*
> *Manila alone,*
> *And then I thought we'd add Luzon;*
> *At last I knelt down in my nightie*
> *And prayed for light to God almighty,*
> *At last I knelt down in my nightie*
> *And prayed for light to God almighty!*

MINISTERS:

> *Praise to our President*
> *In the good Lord confident;*
> *For he knelt down in his nightie*
> *And prayed for light to God almighty!*

MCKINLEY:

> *And this is how it was revealed*
> *to me one midnight;*
> *We could not give them*
> *Back to Spain,*
> *We would be cowards*
> *And profane;*
> *Leave them to Germany*
> *or France?*

Why, Reverend Gentleman, not a chance!
Each one of them is our business rival,
Why, we must think of our survival,
Each one of them is our business rival,
Why, we must think of our survival!

MINISTERS:

Hail to our President
For our commerce provident,
He knows who's our business rival,
And he thinks of our survival!

MCKINLEY:

We could not leave
Them there and quit,
For self-government
They're unfit!
They'd soon have anarchy
And misrule!
So heaven said: "Don't be a fool!
You can't in conscience now forsake them!
I say to you that you must take them!
You can't in conscience now forsake them!
I say to you that you must take them!"

MINISTERS:

Now to our President
This clear message has been sent:
He can't in conscience now forsake them,
God has said that he must take them!

MCKINLEY:

Yes, we must take
Them to civilize,

To educate
And Christianize,
Because for them
Christ also died!
That made me feel so good inside!
And being enlightened thus profoundly,
I went to bed—and slept quite soundly!
And being enlightened thus profoundly,
I went to bed—and slept quite soundly!

MINISTERS:

Thank you, Mr. President,
You have saved our government!
Being enlightened thus profoundly
You deserved to sleep quite soundly!

ALL: Praise be to God!

(The MINISTERS *rise to leave. One of the younger ones approaches* MCKINLEY.*)*

NARRATOR/YOUNG MINISTER: But Mr. President . . .

MCKINLEY: Yes, Reverend?

NARRATOR/YOUNG MINISTER: I understand there are universities in the Philippines that are older than Harvard.

MCKINLEY: *(taken aback)* Eh? *(scowls)* Oh well, yes . . . *(face brightens)* Ah! But they have no public schools!

NARRATOR/YOUNG MINISTER: *(insistent)* And I also understand that ninety percent of the Filipinos are already Christian! In fact, there are proportionally

more baptized persons in that country than right
here in America!

MCKINLEY: *(trying not to look annoyed)* Oh? Yes
. . . Christians . . . *(face brightens again)* Catholics!
Catholics, really—and some of that folk Catholicism
must go. It's retarding progress there. If I may put it
this way, gentlemen: *(sings)*

I got the message at 12:06
We must Christianize the Catholics!

(He winks at the MINISTERS, *who politely, some visibly sourly,
join him in laughter.)*

BLACKOUT

Act Two, Scene 4

NARRATOR: An American army forward command post
near the bridge of San Juan, in the outskirts of
Manila. It is a typical tropic afternoon and the soldiers, most of them with shirts off, are taking it easy.
STICKNEY has been interviewing soldiers.

SOLDIER NO. 1: *(pointing to document under* STICKNEY'S
arm) What's that you're carrying Stickney?

NARRATOR/STICKNEY: This? Oh, this is the full text of
the Treaty of Paris. Came off the wires this morning
(he unfolds document). Signed last December 10.
Makes everything legal.

SOLDIER NO. 2:   What's all legal?

NARRATOR/STICKNEY: Our ownership of the Philippines.

SOLDIER NO. 3:   (*looking across the bridge and spitting tobacco*) Well, if it's all legal why don't *they* lay down their arms and let us take over the country?

NARRATOR/STICKNEY: Because they don't recognize the treaty.

SOLDIER NO. 4:   Why the hell not?

NARRATOR/STICKNEY: Well, in the first place, they were not in on it. They sent their man to Paris, fellow named Agoncillo, but he wasn't even allowed into the Quay d'Orsay.

SOLDIER NO. 5:   The key what?

NARRATOR/STICKNEY: The Quay d'Orsay. It's where the French Foreign Office is. You know, like the State Department.

SOLDIER NO. 6:   But don't these dang people realize we can keep them as war booty?

NARRATOR/STICKNEY: You tell Aguinaldo that. The same treaty gives Cuba back to the Cubans. We get to keep Puerto Rico and Guam gratis. But not the Philippines. For them the treaty provides for twenty millions in compensation to Spain!

SOLDIER NO. 7:   Twenty million dollars!

NARRATOR/STICKNEY: (*tongue in cheek*) I don't really

think that's too much. Considering we're getting ten million people—and seven thousand islands—in exchange! Let's see ... seven thousand islands ... *(counting on his fingers)* twenty million dollars ... that's less than three thousand dollars an island. Ten million people ... twenty million dollars ... Why, that's even better! Two dollars a head! *(sings)*

Two dollars a head!
Two dollars a head!
Money never could that fah go
In the stockyards of Chicago!
Two dollars a head!
Two dollars a head!
Cattle's tasty on the table,
But these men are strong and able,
They won't get consumed like steak,
But for us more wealth they'll make!
Dark and lowly you may think 'em
But they'll raise our national income!
Two dollars a head!
Two dollars a head!

(SOLDIERS *now join to sing and dance*)

SOLDIERS:

Dark and lowly you may think 'em
But they'll raise our national income!
Two dollars a head!
Two dollars a head!

NARRATOR/STICKNEY:

And three thousand for each island
That's a clever way to buy land!

SOLDIERS:

> But ain't that a trifle more
> Than the lousy twenty four
> That we paid for old Manhattan?

NARRATOR/STICKNEY:

> But that land we can't grow fat on,
> All the crop it's good for yielding's
> Tall and very ugly buildings!

SOLDIERS:

> All Manhattan's
> good for yielding's
> Tall and very
> ugly buildings!
>
> Two dollars a head!
> Two dollars a head!

NARRATOR/STICKNEY:

> And three thousand for each island,
> There is flat and low and high land,
> Pregnant all with nature's loot
> And with unforbidden fruit:
> Gold and silver, copper, zinc!
> Our books will never need red ink!

STICKNEY AND SOLDIERS:

> Two dollars a head!
> Two dollars a head!
> It's a bargain don't you think?
> Our books will never need red ink!
> It's a bargain,
> Ain't no arguin'!
> Two dollars a head!

(It is dark as the song and dance ends. Offstage an American voice is heard to shout "Halt!" There is a pause and then another "Halt!" Immediately a Filipino voice replies mockingly "halto!" There is a rifle shot and the agonizing cry of a Filipino falling. There is another "Halt!" and two more shots are fired. There are sounds of more Filipinos falling. An American shouts: "Line up, fellows, the niggers are in here all through these yards!" *The Filipinos begin to return the fire. The battle is on. On stage everyone has been tensely watching.)*

NARRATOR/STICKNEY: February 4, 1899: What we all feared is here. What kind of a war do I report on now? *(he begins to write)* Liberation? Not any more. Counter-insurrection! *(he snaps his finger)* Yes. That would be better! Counter-insurrection. God bless our cause . . .

BLACKOUT

Act Two, Scene 5

NARRATOR: Time: Late 1899. The American front lines in Central Luzon. American dead and wounded are being moved to the rear. EMILIE, now a volunteer nurse, is attending to some of the wounded. BRUMBY, still liaison officer for Dewey, enters with STICKNEY.

BRUMBY: *(sees* EMILIE, *walks up to her)* Emilie!

EMILIE: *(looks up, smiles, obviously weary)* Hello, Tom.

BRUMBY: There's really no need for you to expose yourself like this. The U.S. Army has enough nurses to go around.

EMILIE: I know, Tom. But I just couldn't sit around Manila doing nothing, waiting for a victory that I both wish and fear. Oh, Tom, how much longer is this going to last? It's been over a year. I see no sign of it ending.

BRUMBY: It won't be long now, Emilie. The insurgents will run out of ammunition—or determination —and then we can all go home.

(A troop of SOLDIERS *enter left and march wearily across the stage to exit right. They are singing an authentic derisive song to the tune of "Tramp, tramp, tramp," the army hiking song.)*

SOLDIERS:

> *In the land of dopey dreams*
> *Peaceful, happy Philippines*
> *Where the bolo-man is busy all day long;*
> *Where Americanos die*
> *And the Filipinos lie*
> *And the soldiers sing their army hiking song:*
>
> *Damn, damn, damn the Filipino*
> *Pock-marked khakiac ladrone!*
> *Underneath the starry flag*
> *Civilize him with a krag*
> *And return us to our own beloved home!*

(BRUMBY *and the rest of the* SOLDIERS *are infected by the spirit of the song and take it up.)*

BRUMBY AND SOLDIERS:
> *Damn, damn, damn the Filipino*
> *Pock-marked khakiac ladrone!*
> *Underneath the starry flag*
> *Civilize him with a krag*
> *And return us to our own beloved home!*

EMILIE: *(who has been listening in disgust)* Ladrone? Do you really think these people are robbers? It looks very much like they were just trying to keep their country for themselves!

BRUMBY: *(a little embarrassed)* Oh, it's just a song, Emilie. To keep up the soldiers' morale. These things are necessary in war.

(There is a sudden scream off stage, followed by the sound of gurgling in water.)

NARRATOR: I suppose that is necessary too.

BRUMBY: What was that?

NARRATOR: It's the water cure.

BRUMBY: The what?

NARRATOR: The water cure: It's an—ah—effective way of getting a prisoner to give valuable information.

(There is another scream. More gurgling, drowning sounds. Spot on Senate Investigation Committee; SENATOR LODGE, *chairman; members* SENATORS RAWLINS, BEVERIDGE, *and six other senators.)*

LODGE: Please state your name.

RILEY: Charles S. Riley, 26th Volunteer Infantry.

LODGE: When did you arrive in the Philippine Islands?

RILEY: October 30, 1899.

LODGE: During your service there did you witness what is generally known as the water cure?

RILEY: I did.

LODGE: Where?

RILEY: In the town of Igbaras, Iloilo Province, Panay Island.

LODGE: You may state, Mr. Riley, what you saw in that regard.

RILEY: There was a large galvanized-iron tank, holding probably 100 gallons, about 2 barrels. That was on a raised platform about 10 or 12 inches, I should think, and there was a faucet on the tank. It was the tank we used for catching rainwater for drinking purposes. The presidente . . .

BEVERIDGE: Whom do you mean by the presidente?

RILEY: The head official of the town. He was placed under the tank, and the faucet was opened and a stream of water was forced down or allowed to run down his throat; his throat was held so he could not prevent swallowing the water, so that he had to allow the water to run into his stomach.

NARRATOR: It's really very simple. You repeat the process until he talks.

(Another scream. More gurgling. Then a Filipino voice shouts: "Tama na! Tama na!")

(spot on WILLIAM SMITH*)*

NARRATOR: WILLIAM LEWIS SMITH, 26th Volunteer Infantry.

LODGE: Did you witness what is known as the water cure?

SMITH: Yes, sir.

RAWLINS: Did you observe it inflicted more than once?

SMITH: I saw part of it one time and the whole of it the second time.

LODGE: Describe what you saw on the second occasion.

SMITH: This time it was given by means of a syringe. Two men went out to their saddlebags and obtained two syringes, large bulbs, a common syringe, about 2 feet of common hose pipe, I should think, on either end. One was inserted in his mouth and the other up his nose. When they started into the building, Capt. Glenn was there, and he said, "Don't take him inside, right here is good enough."

(spot on RILEY*)*

RILEY: I was in front of the building, on the sidewalk. A can of water was brought in, what we call a kerosene can, holding about 5 gallons. The presidente was held by four or five men and the water was forced into his mouth from the can, through the syringe. The syringe did not seem to have the desired effect, and the doctor ordered a second syringe, and that was inserted in his nose. Then the doctor ordered some salt, and a handful of salt was thrown into the water. Two syringes were then in operation. The interpreter stood over him in the meantime asking for his second information that was desired. Finally he gave in and gave the information that they sought.

RAWLINS: May I ask the name of the doctor?

RILEY: Dr. Lyons, the contract surgeon.

RAWLINS: An American?

RILEY: Yes, sir.

(spot on GEN. HUGHES*)*

NARRATOR: ROBERT P. HUGHES, Brig. General, U.S. Army, Provost-marshal-general of Manila.

LODGE: If cases of cruelty or oppression toward a prisoner or toward a peaceably-disposed native occured, were the men tried and punished?

HUGHES: They certainly would have been. The point is this: I cannot say there were no such cases, because that would be one of the things that would meet with immediate action on my part, and if they occurred they would not let me know it if they could help it, and there may have been occasional cases of it without my knowledge. However, I never knew of any case in all my two years and a half in the Department of Visayas.

(spot on RILEY*)*

SEN. NO. 1:   Mr. Riley, were there any officers present during the process?

RILEY: Yes, sir. Capt. Glenn, our commanding officer walked back and forth from one room to the other, and went in two or three times.

(spot on SMITH*)*

SMITH: When they started taking the men into the building, Capt. Glenn said, "Don't take him inside. Right here is good enough."

(spot on RILEY*)*

SEN. NO. 2:   Was Capt. Glenn judge-advocate under Gen. Hughes?

RILEY: Yes, that was Gen. Hughes' Department.

(spot on MANNING*)*

NARRATOR: JANUARIUS MANNING, First Sergeant, 26th Volunteer Infantry.

LODGE: What part of the Philippine Islands were you in?

MANNING: In the island of Panay, province of Iloilo.

LODGE: In Gen. Hughes' division?

MANNING: Yes, sir.

SEN. NO. 3:   Were you a witness while you were there to

any cruelty or torture of the natives, any application of the water cure?

MANNING: Yes, sir. I saw the water cure.

SEN. NO. 4:   Were you engaged in it?

MANNING: Well, I was there. I didn't give it myself; I directed the men to do it.

RAWLINS: Did you receive orders from anyone to do that?

MANNING: Yes, sir. The commanding officer, Capt. Gregg.

(spot on GIBBS*)*

NARRATOR: WILLIAM J. GIBBS, 26th Volunteer Infantry.

BEVERIDGE: You said you had not seen the water cure administered, but you had seen the water brought in.

GIBBS: Yes, sir. Some of my comrades and myself tried to peep in the windows and see what was going on. We could hear a good many things.

SEN. NO. 5:   What did you hear?

GIBBS: We heard moans from the men which I expect were getting the water cure, and then we could see a kind of sickly expression on a man's face after coming out.

(spot on OTIS*)*

NARRATOR: MAJOR-GENERAL ELWELL S. OTIS, Military

Governor of the Philippine Islands, August to May, 1900.

BEVERIDGE: Will you tell the Committee what the fact is about the cruelty toward the natives, prisoners or otherwise, of American officers and soldiers; as to whether cruelty by American officers and soldiers was practiced upon the people, or even upon prisoners, or whether, on the contrary, kindness and consideration was practiced by our troops toward them?

OTIS: The greatest kindness.

(spot on MANNING)

SEN. NO. 6: What did they put in his mouth to keep it open?

MANNING: A stick, generally; a small stick would be put in his mouth to keep it open; a little piece of stick, so he could not close it up. Then the water would be poured down, and when he would breathe of course he would have to take in the water.

(spot on RILEY)

SEN. NO. 1: Do I understand you to say that he was put to this torture to compel him to give evidence against himself?

RILEY: Yes, sir.

(spot on COL. WAGNER)

NARRATOR: COL. ARTHUR L. WAGNER, Asst. Adjutant-general, U.S. Army.

SEN. NO. 2:   I will ask you if you are familiar enough with the so-called water cure to state whether or not that would be authorized by the rules of war?

WAGNER: Well, sir, I am not familiar with the water cure; I never saw it applied; I have never even seen a thorough description of it. I have never heard of any case of death resulting from it.

(spot on RILEY)

BEVERIDGE: Did anybody kill him?

RILEY: Kill whom, the Doctor?

BEVERIDGE: Yes.

RILEY: No, sir.

(spot on FUNSTON)

NARRATOR: FREDERICK FUNSTON, Brig. Gen. U.S. Army.

FUNSTON: During my service of three years in the Philippines I never had personal knowledge of the so-called water cure being administered to a native, or any other form of torture being used to extract information from them. The so-called water cure was by no means so severe an ordeal. The method was merely to throw a native on his back, hold his nose with one hand, and pour water down his throat from a canteen or other vessel. It occasioned nothing more than a few moments of strangling and never resulted fatally.

(spot on GIBBS)

SEN. NO. 3: What do you know of the results of this water cure?

GIBBS: One man died in Catbalogan.

SEN. NO. 4: Who was that?

GIBBS: I don't know his name.

(spot on RILEY)

RAWLINS: What was done with the town of Igbaras?

RILEY: The town was burned.

RAWLINS: By whose order?

RILEY: By order of Capt. Glenn.

RAWLINS: How many houses were destroyed?

RILEY: Practically the entire town.

SEN. NO. 5: How were those houses occupied?

RILEY: They were occupied with native families.

LODGE: Men, women, and children?

RILEY: Men, women, and children; yes, sir.

RAWLINS: Do you know what reason, if any, was assigned for burning the town?

RILEY: On account of the information obtained by the water cure treatment that morning.

(spot on GEN. ARTHUR MACARTHUR)

NARRATOR: ARTHUR MACARTHUR, Major General, U.S. Army, military governor of the Philippine Islands from May 1900 to July 1901.

BEVERIDGE: The general conduct of our soldiers and officers in the Philippine Islands, irrespective of orders from headquarters, was in the direction of kindness, mercy, and humanity, wasn't it?

MACARTHUR: Absolutely, sir.

BEVERIDGE: Instead of the reverse?

MACARTHUR: The bearing of our Army as a whole was simply superb.

(There is silence. Spot returns to BRUMBY *and* EMILIE, *who is staring blankly and numbly forward.)*

BRUMBY: Emilie once said to me in Manila that this was not the way she had seen this all. Is this the way I saw it when I volunteered to join the Asiatic Squadron?

NARRATOR: It would appear that the American conscience is beginning to get disturbed.

BLACKOUT

Act Two, Scene 6

NARRATOR: The war dragged on. The Filipinos pinned their hopes on the Presidential elections of 1900. They were sure that the Democratic candidate, William Jennings Bryan, would defeat McKinley and would pull American troops out of the Philippines.

(The 1900 presidential campaign. There is a crowd facing backstage listening to the speakers. There are two platforms on either side, each under a huge campaign poster. The one on the left reads: "DEMOCRATIC PARTY—FOR PRESIDENT—WILLIAM JENNINGS BRYAN; FOR VICE-PRESIDENT—ADLAI E. STEVENSON." *The one on the right reads:* "REPUBLICAN PARTY—FOR PRESIDENT—WILLIAM MCKINLEY; FOR VICE-PRESIDENT—THEODORE ROOSVELT." *The stage is in semi-darkness. The spotlight is on the right platform from which* MCKINLEY *is about to speak.)*

MCKINLEY: It was a difficult decision. But now that I have made it, you are seeing its wisdom and its fruits. Our industries were producing more than the home market could consume. Now, the people of Puerto Rico, Guam, and the Philippines are our new markets. And, furthermore, the Philippines are our gateway to China. They are our gateway to the world!

(Cheers. Spotlight moves left to BRYAN.*)*

BRYAN: I will not develop markets overseas by trampling on the dignity of the smaller nations. Instead, I will raise your purchasing power—you Americans—so that you can buy more and more of the products of our industry! *(cheers)* Imperialism! Imperialism is the issue in these elections!

(Cheers. Spotlight is back on MCKINLEY.*)*

MCKINLEY: There is nothing even remotely resembling imperialism in our policy. Expansionism is not imperialism.

(Cheers. Spotlight is back on BRYAN.*)*

BRYAN: Imperialism! Imperialism brings with it militarism which means a gigantic expenditure of the taxpayers' money everywhere except in his own home!
(Cheers. Spotlight back on right this time revealing THEODORE ROOSEVELT. *More cheers.)*

ROOSEVELT: Bryanist democracy is the most dangerous foe of our soldiers who are facing death. The Tagal bandit in Luzon will stop killing our soldiers very soon after he becomes convinced that he will receive no aid from the party of which Mr. Bryan is chief. Mr. Bryan calls us militarists and tyrants. Will all men in uniform in this assembly raise your hands?

(uniformed men raise hands)

ROOSEVELT: Behold your tyrants!

(Wild cheers. Spotlight back on BRYAN.*)*

BRYAN: Our forefathers fought for independence under a banner upon which was inscribed: "Millions for defense but not a cent for tribute!" And so those who today not only desire American independence but are willing to encourage the idea of independence in other races can fight under a banner upon which is inscribed a similar motto: "Millions for defense, but not one cent for conquest!"

(Cheers. Spotlight back on ROOSEVELT.*)*

ROOSEVELT: These Democrats loudly demand self-government for Tagalog bandits while they are conniving at the denial of the right of self-government to our fellow Americans of dusky color in North Carolina. Bryan says we Republicans are concerned only with money and ignore human rights. He has no right to speak of those rights at all until he is willing to denounce the wrong to the black man in North Carolina, and with at least the fervor he uses in denouncing the wholly imaginary wrongs done to the brown man in the Philippines!

(Cheers. Spotlight back on BRYAN.*)*

BRYAN: The other issue in this campaign is—silver and gold!

(The CROWD *look at each other, surprised at this switch to a boring subject.)*

I am for bimetallism. If they dare to come out in the open field and defend the gold standard as a good thing, we will fight them to the uttermost. Having behind us the producing masses of this nation and the world, we will answer their demand for a gold standard by saying to them: You shall not press down upon the brow of labor this crown of thorns, you shall not crucify mankind upon a cross of gold!

(Light applause. Stage darkens. The spotlight is now on STICKNEY *at his desk typing a letter to Brumby.)*

NARRATOR/STICKNEY: *(reading)* Dear Tom, when you read this you will have known for a month now that

McKinley has been reelected. Dewey's announcement of his availability never caught fire. One count against him was that his wife, whom he recently married, is Catholic.

(Stage brightens. DEWEY *is with his old* Olympia STAFF; BRUMBY *and* GRIDLEY *are not present.)*

DEWEY: Gentlemen, for many years during my residence in Washington before going to the Pacific, I had a most charming lady friend, a widow, Mrs. Mildred McLean Hazen. Gentlemen, I thought you should be the first to know that Mrs. Hazen, Mildred, has done me the honor of accepting my hand in marriage.

OFFICERS: Well! Congratulations! Well done, sir! Best wishes!

LAMBERTON: It took her a little longer than Spain to surrender, eh, Admiral! *(laughter)*

DEWEY: Yes . . . well, I didn't have Aguinaldo to help me! *(more laughter)*

LAMBERTON: I've heard of Mrs. Hazen. Handsome woman, I understand. She's about . . . oh, forty-nine?

NARRATOR/STICKNEY: Yes, and the Admiral is 62.

(The OFFICERS *look at each other with naughty, dubious looks.)*

NARRATOR/STICKNEY: Well, why not?

LAMBERTON: Well . . . *(sings)*

After the Admiral had once
Retired from those islands,
I thought that like the Olympia's *guns*
His would now be silenced!

       (mischievous laughter)

NARRATOR/STICKNEY:

I hope you're not suggesting, sir,
That it is your suspicion
That at his age the Admiral here
Has no more ammunition!

You are unscientific, sir,
And poor in your biology,
And you don't seem a whit to care
For the science of histology!

LAMBERTON: You mean history, Joe.

NARRATOR/STICKNEY: No, sir, histology—that branch of biology concerned with the microscopic study of the structure of tissues!

LAMBERTON: Oh.

NARRATOR/STICKNEY:

But if you will insist on some
Historical assessment,
I will begin with samples from
The pages of the Test'ment!

Now, there was the aged King Boaz.
He married a widow to show us
That the old can still save it,
For out came King David
Among his spermatozoas!

LAMBERTON: *(in mock pain)* Ohhh!

NARRATOR/STICKNEY: You must forgive the poetic license, of course. The plural of spermatozoon is spermatozoa, not zoas!

LAMBERTON: Thank you!

NARRATOR/STICKNEY: You're welcome!

REES: *(cutting in, as it were)*

> *King David when in his stoopin' age*
> *Took young Abishag in concubinage;*
> *When he died his son made room*
> *For her in his baid room*
> *Because she was still in whoopeein' age!*

LAMBERTON: *(in mock disgust)* Ohhh!

NARRATOR/STICKNEY:

> *When Sarah was sixty plus thrice X*
> *(That's ninety!) she thought 'twas good-by sex!*
> *Even older was Abie,*
> *But he wanted a baby*
> *So out came the first of the Isaacs!*

LAMBERTON: *(in mock despair)* No!

REES:

> *At eight hundred years, old Methuselah*
> *He did many things that aren't usuallah*
> *Associated with those*
> *Whose arrows and bows*
> *Do no more but hang around looselah!*

LAMBERTON: *(now getting into the spirit)* Let's leave the

Bible for a moment. How about a little classical history?

When Caesar became rather itchy
And Cleo obligingly bitchy,
An old man he was rated
Yet she got impregnated!
He veni and vidi and vici!

NARRATOR/STICKNEY: *Vivat!*

The girl Louis Fifteenth did marry
Was older but quite voluptuary;
Seven children got he
Then at age sixty-three
He was at it with Madame du Barry!

REES: *Très bon!*

That same King Louis thought it foxy
A contagiously ill girl to unfrock, see,
So at seventy-seven
He went up to heaven.

(He gestures up. LAMBERTON shakes his head sadly and points down.)

Not because he was sexy but poxy!

NARRATOR/STICKNEY: *Formidable!*

LAMBERTON:

The Englishman Henry the Eighth
The Pope called "Defender of the Faith";
He defended his creed
With six women to breed
And until he dieth he laith!

REES: Jolly good! But sirs, Admiral Dewey is American.
Have we no precedents in our history?

NARRATOR/STICKNEY: Our precedents, if you will pardon the pun, are our Presidents!

Now William Henry Harrison
He had ten children fine;
He had almost bred a garrison
When he died at eighty-nine!

John Tyler's first wife bore
Eight children—cute, they reckoned,
He wanted more at fifty-four,
Had seven by his second!

LAMBERTON: I studied U.S. history too!

Buchanan was a bache-lor,
An object of derision,
Did they his manhood doubt or
That darned Dred Scott decision!

Grover Cleveland at nine and forty
At the White House married;
And following this late late sortie
His wife five babies carried!

REES:

And there was Benjamin Harrison
Who wed at sixty-three;
He didn't breed a garrison,
But one darling child had he!

And so you see to marry late
Is really not idiotic;
I think in fact that we should rate
The action quite patriotic!

ALL:
> *And so you see to marry late*
> *Is really not idiotic;*
> *We think in fact that we should rate*
> *The action quite patriotic!*

DEWEY: *(laughing heartily)* Gentlemen, I want you to be the first to know. I have made the decision to hold myself available for nomination for candidacy for President of the United States. If the American people want me for this high office, I shall only be too willing to serve them.

(spot on ROOSEVELT*)*

ROOSEVELT: Fellow Americans, it is my honor as Governor of New York to present this Tiffany loving cup of solid gold embossed with sketches of his victories to the spearhead of America's destiny —George Dewey.

DEWEY: I am proud to accept this from the architect of that destiny—Theodore Roosevelt.

(spot on MCKINLEY*)*

MCKINLEY: The Congress has authorized me, as your President, and I quote, to appoint by selection and promotion an Admiral of the Navy, who shall not be placed upon the retired list by his own application; and whenever such office shall be vacated by death or otherwise, the office shall cease to exist. It is my understanding, my fellow countrymen, that this permanent and unretirable promotion was intended by Congress—and I heartily concur with that intent—to apply to Admiral George E. Dewey!

(stage brightens)

NARRATOR/STICKNEY: Admiral, do you feel that your naval background, however brilliant, is proper —er—sufficient qualification for the Presidency?

DEWEY: *(somewhat militant and indignant)* Since studying the subject I am convinced that the office of the President is not such a very difficult one to fill. His duties are mainly to execute the laws of Congress.

NARRATOR/STICKNEY: *(trying to seem encouraging)* Which party convention would you try for, Admiral?

DEWEY: I am available for any party.

NARRATOR/STICKNEY: But, sir, on what platform will you stand?

DEWEY: Platform? Well—uh—I think I have said enough at this time and *(looking around and noticing no real enthusiasm)* and possibly too much.

(spot on STICKNEY)

NARRATOR/STICKNEY: Dear Tom, when you read this you will have known for a month now that McKinley has been reelected. Dewey's announcement of his availability never caught fire. One count against him was that his wife whom he recently married is Catholic, and there was fear that her home in Washington, the one the government gave Dewey as a prize, might become the official seat of the Papacy in the District of Columbia. Besides her gowns and jewels were excessively grand and ostentatious. Bryan lost by an electoral vote of 292 to 155. The election issues . . .

(spot on BRUMBY*)*

BRUMBY: The election issues were garbled. Bryan made
the mistake of introducing the tired old issue of the
gold standard. The issue of imperialism was lost in
the confusion. Theodore Roosevelt was a most effective campaigner. With his and McKinley's victory, anti-imperialism is as good as dead.

(There are shouts of joy offstage. BRUMBY *turns to listen. Some
sailors and soldiers, a little drunk, enter left.* BRUMBY *stops a
sailor.)*

BRUMBY: What's all the shouting about, sailor?

SAILOR: Haven't you heard, sir? Aguinaldo has been
captured—in the hills up north, tricked with
Filipino mercenaries. The war is over! *(exits right with
others)*

BRUMBY: Yeah, the war is over *(he crushes Stickney's letter in his hand in cynical gesture.)*

BLACKOUT

Act Two, Scene 7

WILLIAMS: Tom, I called for you to inform you that you
are to join our party to welcome the U.S. transport
Thomas when it docks tomorrow.

BRUMBY: The transport *Thomas?* Why? Who's arriving
on it that's so special?

WILLIAMS: Schoolteachers.

BRUMBY: Schoolteachers?

WILLIAMS: Yes, schoolteachers! Hundreds of them! And some doctors, malaria experts—and nurses. It's a new kind of army. A Peace Army. Someday someone will think of an even snappier name than that. For now, Peace Army should do!

BRUMBY: *(pensively)* Yes, it should do. But will it undo what has been done?

WILLIAMS: What do you mean?

BRUMBY: The killing, the deceiving, the rescuing *(sarcastically)* of these people from the jaws of independence.

WILLIAMS: Brumby, you're beginning to talk like Emilie! *(recovering)* And you're both right. I have had my own feelings about all this and I have not hidden them from you. But it's all over, Brumby. We have to face realities. McKinley has been reelected. The American people have spoken. Aguinaldo has fallen. Now that I'm with the Governor's office, I get the wider picture more clearly. There's nothing left but to help rebuild this country.

BRUMBY: *(now somewhat resigned)* And let the American conscience speak up—with a little squeak.

WILLIAMS: Yes, all right, with a little squeak . . . until it regains its full voice . . . and *(gravely)* gives back to these people all—or some—of what we're taking away.

NARRATOR: The gangplank of the transport *U.S.S. Thomas*. Teachers, doctors, nurses, bags in hand, some already dressed in tropical white, others still in darker U.S. clothes, are coming off the ship. WILLIAMS, BRUMBY and high American officials are welcoming them. EMILIE watches backstage with some lady friends.

WILLIAMS: In the name of the Military Governor, I welcome you to the Philippines, Ladies and Gentlemen.

(some grateful murmurs of "thank you," "glad to be here")

BRUMBY: *(to a woman teacher arrival)* I am Lieutenant Brumby, m'am. Welcome. What part of the States are you from?

TEACHER 1:   Ithaca, New York.

BRUMBY: Oh? And you m'am?

TEACHER 2:   Ames, Iowa.

BRUMBY: Well, you come from all over, don't you?

TEACHER 1:   Young man, it's good talking to you but will you show us to the superintendent? We're eager to get our assignments.

BRUMBY: But m'am, with all this tropic heat, don't you want to rest awhile before thinking of assignments?

TEACHER 2:   This heat's no worse than Iowa in the summer. We've come to get a job done—not to rest!

BRUMBY: *(embarrassed)* Yes, yes, of course *(looks around)*. Oh, there he is. There's your superintendent—Mr.

Atkins. *(The teachers go up to* ATKINS. BRUMBY *is pensive. He sees* EMILIE *and goes to her.)* Emilie!

EMILIE: *(who has been warmer to* BRUMBY *since the water cure incident)* Hello, Tom.

BRUMBY: Emilie, I came here today ready to be cynical about this whole Peace Army business. But I'm beginning to wonder. Can it work? Is it possible? *(sings)*

Is it possible
After you've slapped your neighbor
To offer him your hand?
Is it possible
After you've knocked him down
To pull him back to stand?

EMILIE:

It is possible
After you've slapped your neighbor
Your hand he may reject!
Or you may have
Knocked him down so hard
He'll no longer stand erect!

BRUMBY AND EMILIE:

You can cure his body,
Train his mind or steer it.
But what are we to do
About his spirit?

Is it possible
To start doing just that
And stop asking why?
There is really
Nothing much left for us
To do but try!

BRUMBY: Emilie, I'm going to give it a try!

EMILIE: How, Tom?

BRUMBY: I . . . I *(with decision)* I'm resigning my commission in the Navy and applying to be a schoolteacher!

EMILIE: *(overwhelmed)* Tom!

BRUMBY: And I'm going to ask for an assignment in the remotest barrio!

EMILIE: *(now completely devastated and going limp)* Darling!

BRUMBY: *(rushes to hold her up)* Emilie!

EMILIE: Darling, do you think . . . do you think the Department of Education might have room for just one more teacher, a certain Mrs. T.F. Brumby?

(They kiss.)

CURTAIN

Act Two, Scene 8

NARRATOR: The front yard of a nipa house in a barrio in Central Luzon. BRUMBY and EMILIE, now married, have been living in it and teaching in the barrio school. BRUMBY is seated on the front steps preparing a lesson plan.

BRUMBY: *(throwing down his pencil in good-natured despera-tion)* Oh, what's the use *(he looks up at the house)*. Emilie!

EMILIE: *(from inside the house)* Yes, Tom?

BRUMBY: Wouldn't it have been simpler if our government had just decided to continue teaching these kids Spanish. After all, they've had it for almost four hundred years.

EMILIE: *(looking out the window)* Not all of them, Tom. The Spaniards never really wanted all the Filipinos to learn Spanish.

BRUMBY: Why not?

EMILIE: Well, maybe they didn't want them to be able to read too many books about progress in Europe. Besides, where would we be if everything had to be taught in Spanish? How could we carry out our *(she smiles)* manifest destiny?

(BRUMBY *smiles back and blows* EMILIE *a kiss. She disappears back into the house. Two Americans,* BILL CARSON *and* JACK O'MALLEY, *obviously weary with travel, in straw hats, white suits and carrying carpet bags, enter left.)*

BRUMBY: Hullo. What have we here? Fellow Yankees in barrio San Roque? Good morning, gentlemen.

CARSON: *(mopping his forehead)* Mornin'!

BRUMBY: But where do you . . . how did you . . . ?

O'MALLEY: We're businessmen, sir. We got off the train from Manila about ten miles back. Thought we'd size up the country a bit.

BRUMBY: Well, sit ye down and have a rest, friends.

CARSON: Thanks.

BRUMBY: You just come from Manila? What's new at the capital?

O'MALLEY: Here *(handing* BRUMBY *a newspaper).* Today's *Manila Times.*

BRUMBY: Thanks. *(Sits down to read. He jumps up suddenly.)* Holy Moses!

EMILIE: *(looking out the window)* What's the matter? *(*CARSON *and* O'MALLEY *rise)*

BRUMBY: Oh, I'm sorry. These gentlemen are businessmen. They've just come in from Manila. Gentlemen, this is my wife, Emilie. And I'm Tom Brumby. We're schoolteachers here.

CARSON: Bill Carson, m'am, at your service.

O'MALLEY: And I'm Jack O'Malley.

EMILIE: How do you do, gentlemen. Please, do sit down. *(to* BRUMBY*)* Tom, what on earth were you shouting about?

BRUMBY: Come down and I'll show you! *(*EMILIE *comes down)* Look! It says President . . . President Roosevelt retains most of McKinley Cabinet. President Roosevelt?

CARSON: Guess you folks haven't heard. McKinley was shot in Buffalo a couple of weeks ago by some anarchist named Leon Czol . . . something. Died a few days later.

BRUMBY: Well . . . *(to himself)* at least Theodore Roosevelt got to *his* destiny *(to* EMILIE*)* But Emilie, we're being rude to our guests. They need something to cool off with. How about some nice calamansi juice.

EMILIE: Of course *(goes up to the house)*

CARSON: Excuse me, what was that juice, again?

BRUMBY: Calamansi. It's a small, very juicy citrus fruit. The juice is a concentrate. You add sugar and water to it. Sorry we have no ice.

(EMILIE *comes down from house and serves.*)

CARSON: *(tasting)* Delicious!

O'MALLEY: Mmm—yes. Might even be better if it were carbonated.

EMILIE: I'm sure it would. Maybe some enterprising American businessmen might want to set up a bottling plant for calamansi soda pop!

CARSON: Oh that's already on the planning stage, m'am. O'Malley's outfit is setting one up just outside Manila.

EMILIE: Oh?

O'MALLEY: Yeah. We're bringing in the secret concentrate from Atlanta, Georgia, and some old bottling machines from California. Then we're getting a loan from the Manila Archbishop's bank. And with gallons of free Philippine water and good, cheap, local labor, we're in business!

EMILIE: But why don't you use local fruit juices?

O'MALLEY: Well, for one thing, you couldn't get a steady supply . . .

CARSON: Why don't you tell her the real story, Jack. M'am, the fastest growing soft drink corporation in America would gang up with other American manufacturers and kick up the biggest row you ever heard and Jack here would be sent packing home tomorrow if they as much as suspected that we're not going to be exporting their products here—and duty free, too!

EMILIE: *(now getting visibly angry)* Duty free?

CARSON: Yeah. That's what's known as "free trade." Imports are duty free both ways.

(EMILIE is now speechless with anger.)

BRUMBY: *(trying to relieve the tension)* And are you in the soda pop business too, Mr. Carson?

CARSON: Oh no. I'm in sardines.

BRUMBY: Sardines?

CARSON: Yes, sardines from the canneries of Seattle and Monterrey. I'm going around the countryside surveying the market.

BRUMBY: But, Mr. Carson, the Philippine waters are teeming with fish. Why not just show these people how to make better catches? You've heard the saying: Give a man a fish and he will eat for a day; show him how to fish and he will eat all his life.

CARSON: My dear, Mr. Brumby, where were you when the last war was being fought?

BRUMBY: I was in the navy, sir *(getting indignant)*.

CARSON: Oh? Well, where were you when the war *(he winks at* O'MALLEY *who winks back)* was being planned? *(*BRUMBY *is stumped. He looks guiltily at* EMILIE. *He recovers and then begins to sing a little unsurely.)*

BRUMBY:

Yes give a man a fish
And he will eat for a day;
But show him how to fish
And he will eat all the way!

CARSON:

That may all be true,
But, Mr. Brumby, you
Are missing the point, and I'm telling it,
Mr. Brumby, I wish
We could give them the fish,
But that's not my job, I am selling it!

EMILIE:

These people of initiative
You will rob!

CARSON:

But for many an American
We're creating a job!

O'MALLEY:

These people you teach
To be Yankees in speech
And to swallow ideas of freedom;
Our mission from God it is
To sell them commodities
Even if they in fact may not need 'em!

CARSON:

> *Our sales talk, they'll love it!*
> *Our products they'll covet!*
> *They'll rush for the mail order* caht-*alogue!*
> *Then we'll draw from their soil*
> *Their gold, maybe oil,*
> *And timber of which they've a lot to log!*

EMILIE:

> *They'll be hewers of wood,*
> *They'll be water haulers!*

CARSON:

> *But, madam, remember*
> *We'll pay them in dollars!*

BRUMBY:

> *But you'll only make rich*
> *A few families which*
> *Are owners, and they are a cozy list!*

O'MALLEY:

> *For shame, sir, for shame*
> *Where I come from the name*
> *For you would be—dirty socialist!*

CARSON AND O'MALLEY:

> *(faking a vaudeville exit step with their straw hats)*

> *For shame, sir, for shame,*
> *Where we come from the name*
> *For you would be—dirty socialist!*

(EMILIE *goes up to the house in disgust.* BRUMBY *starts to go after her but changes his mind.*)

CARSON: *(embracing* BRUMBY) I hope you didn't take that too seriously, Mr. Brumby *(looking up at the house).* I'm afraid Mrs. Brumby did. We were just having a little fun.

BRUMBY: It's all right, gentlemen. I guess . . . I guess it's just that you and us . . . we seem to represent two opposite points of view among Americans—the moral and the practical.

O'MALLEY: Well, it's a free country, Mr. Brumby.

CARSON: Yeah, free to choose what point of view it wants, too, and I'm afraid the American people made their choice when they reelected McKinley. And with Mr. Roosevelt in the White House, it's final.

BRUMBY: Final? *(he looks up to house wanting to join* EMILIE) Final? I wonder. There are many countries in Asia, Mr. Carson. Now that America has gotten started, there will be other confrontations between your point of view and *(looking up at the house again)* and ours. I think the American people will have to be making the choice over and over again.

O'MALLEY: Then why don't we all just wait till the next time? In the meantime, let's all accept the decision now. It's there!

BRUMBY: *(slowly)* No. No. I won't. We won't. We'll fight! Now! *(he rushes up to the house)* Emilie!

CURTAIN

Act Two, Scene 9

NARRATOR: The outer office of the Military Governor.
BRUMBY and EMILIE are seated, nervously waiting,
watching the door to the inner office. There is some
shouting inside. The door opens. WILLIAMS enters,
downcast, looks sadly at EMILIE.

EMILIE: Well, daddy?

WILLIAMS: I'm sorry, Emilie. General MacArthur
. . . the Military Governor is too busy. He can't see
you.

BRUMBY: Did you show him our petition?

WILLIAMS: Yes.

EMILIE: Did he read it?

WILLIAMS: Yes, Emilie, he read it.

EMILIE: Well?

WILLIAMS: *(hesitatingly)* Emilie, he thinks you and Tom
are doing a wonderful job in your barrio school.

EMILIE: That's nice to hear, but what about the petition?

WILLIAMS: Yes, well . . . the general appreciates your
concern over business and trade. But he thinks your
job is education, not business. Let businessmen
worry about business.

BRUMBY: But, sir, we're supposed to teach these people
about the generosity of the great American Republic. How can we do that while we watch them exploited by our . . . our carpetbaggers?

WILLIAMS: Tom, why take up a fight the Filipinos themselves don't care for? There are only a handful of
radicals and anarchists who . . .

EMILIE: Father! You don't really believe that! You know
Apolinario Mabini, for instance. You know he's no
anarchist. He's a patriot and a statesman. Why is he
still in prison?

WILLIAMS: He . . . he has no money. So he prefers to
stay in prison.

BRUMBY: No! *(incredulous)*

WILLIAMS: I swear that's the truth. Tom, sit down. Let
me explain to you what's happening. Businessmen
want order and stability. They can't do business
otherwise. And the army is tired of fighting. They
want order and stability too.

BRUMBY: But what does our petition for an investigation of our economic policies have to do with order
and stability?

WILLIAMS: *(half-exasperated)* You're rocking the boat,
Tom, my son. That's what it amounts to. You're
rocking the boat!

BRUMBY: But, sir, I thought we were trying to teach
these people democracy. How about the right to
speak?

WILLIAMS: The general feels that right must be suspended when order and stability demand it. Son
(now fully exasperated), there's a proclamation on the
general's desk which he is about to sign! It declares
martial law! All those opposed to cooperating with
the government will be imprisoned! The press will

be censored! And Mabini and his friends are being deported to Guam!

(EMILIE *and* BRUMBY *stare at each other, stunned.*)

BRUMBY: *(slowly)* Let's go, Emilie. Our little barrio is waiting. At least we still have our own little dream democratic world waiting.

(EMILIE *kisses her father and starts to leave with* BRUMBY)

WILLIAMS: Emilie . . . (EMILIE *and* BRUMBY *look back*) I . . . I . . . *(very painfully)* I am afraid even your own little dream democratic world is gone.

EMILIE: What? What are you saying?

WILLIAMS: The general feels that with your—er—ideas your continued presence even in a little barrio could be—uh—subversive of the constituted government.

EMILIE: Oh?

WILLIAMS: He therefore suggests very strongly that you both resign your positions.

BRUMBY: *(angrily)* No!

WILLIAMS: And that *(almost tearfully)* you both sail for home in the next available transport *(he goes to* EMILIE *who is now weeping and embraces her).* It won't be so bad, Emilie. We have all been too long away from home, anyway. I'm retiring soon myself. Maybe back home we can ask our questions. *(To* BRUMBY*)* Maybe you can go and ask your friend Teddy your questions. Then maybe you'll get answers. If *he* can't give them, who can?

CURTAIN

Act Two, Scene 10

NARRATOR: The office of President Theodore Roosevelt at the White House. BRUMBY and EMILIE are seated on a sofa. ROOSEVELT is standing in front of his desk leaning on it. He starts to pace the floor as he speaks.

ROOSEVELT: Even if you hadn't asked to see me, I would have sent for you, Brumby. I hadn't really lost track of you since that day you volunteered to join Dewey. The Navy Department has kept me posted.

BRUMBY: Thank you, Mr. President.

(There's an awkward silence as ROOSEVELT *continues to pace the floor pensively.)*

ROOSEVELT: And your father, Mrs. Brumby. I know of his good work. He strikes me as a fine example of a colonial officer, a bit after the British tradition.

EMILIE: Thank you, sir.

BRUMBY: Are we establishing a colonial office, Mr. President?

ROOSEVELT: A colonial office? No, no, the Department of the Interior can handle Philippine affairs very well indeed. Besides, putting up a colonial office would make the whole thing sound so . . . so permanent *(he looks pensively out the window).*

BRUMBY: *(tentatively)* Are you . . . also . . . changing your mind about manifest destiny, Mr. President?

ROOSEVELT: Eh? Oh, no. Of course not, Brumby. A

nation must pursue its destiny or be lost. But sometimes destiny has to be—uh—redirected.

BRUMBY: *(after exchanging a look with* EMILIE*)* I don't understand, sir.

ROOSEVELT: I was reading a newspaper the other day, *The Springfield Republican.* It said that only one person in ten in this country is taking the slightest interest in the Philippines. Only ten thousand Americans out of our eighty million population continue to read about the Philippines. Brumby, it's getting increasingly difficult to get our people even to remember those islands.

EMILIE: Yes, Mr. President, but in the meantime *(getting bolder)* are they to be exploited?

ROOSEVELT: Now, now, Mrs. Brumby. I know you've had a bitter experience over there. And I'm sorry it turned out for you and Brumby the way it did. But we have to be patient. Sometimes the wheels of destiny can roll very slowly. Now as you see I've sent none other than William Howard Taft as first civil governor there. Military governors can be so . . . so military! *(He smiles and manages to make* EMILIE *smile.)*

BRUMBY: May I go back to the "non-permanent" colonial destiny, Mr. President? Are you saying we are not in the Philippines for good?

ROOSEVELT: I wrote to Governor Taft the other day. I don't mind telling you in confidence what I said to him. I said the Philippines now form our heel of Achilles, that they are all that makes the present situation with Japan dangerous. I said to him that personally I should be glad to see the islands independent *(he notices the look of surprised satisfaction on* BRUMBY *and* EMILIE*)* with perhaps some kind of international guarantee for the preservation of order. I would rather see America fight all her life than to see her give up the Philippines to Japan under duress!

BRUMBY: If we keep treating the Filipinos the way we are today, they might just be eager to surrender to the Japanese.

ROOSEVELT: I rather doubt that, Brumby. I've been re-reading Philippine history. I see now that these Filipinos were fighting the Spaniards for their freedom before we ever fought the British for ours. We will treat them better, encourage their democracy, and if the Japanese ever come down to Southeast Asia I predict they'll find the Filipinos will be their toughest customers. *And* the Filipinos may dislike General Otis or General MacArthur today, but they may be hailing other General Otises or MacArthurs as liberators tomorrow!

EMILIE: *(now determined to press the subject)* Yes, Mr. President. But in the meantime, what is to be done about the American businessmen who are out to squeeze the islands dry?

ROOSEVELT: Ah, yes, the businessmen. There are all kinds of them, Mrs. Brumby. Do you know that many big businessmen were opposed to our war with Spain and our invasion of the Philippines? They said it would disturb world stability and be bad for business. Now some of these same businessmen are going to make it hard for us to give the Philippines their independence!

EMILIE: But will you . . .

ROOSEVELT: *(cutting her off)* Mind you, I have nothing against our businessmen. They may not be the backbone of the nation but they make the nation move. I am *(getting somewhat oratorical)* against those malefactors of great wealth, the monopolists, the men who trample on labor, who seek gain, not by genuine work, but by gambling. There you have the new foes of our destiny, Mrs. Brumby. Subdue them and you may be solving the very problems that you left behind in the Philippines.

(SECRETARY *enters*)

SECRETARY: Senator Lodge is here, Mr. President.

ROOSEVELT: Oh? Show him in *(smiles at* BRUMBY*)*. This is going to be quite a reunion. Mrs. Brumby, has your husband told you about that memorable afternoon that winter at the Navy Department?

EMILIE: *(respectful but not enthusiastic)* Yes, Mr. President.

(LODGE *enters left*)

ROOSEVELT: Cabot!

LODGE: Mr. President! *(they shake hands)*

ROOSEVELT: *(placing arm around* BRUMBY*)* Cabot, you remember Brumby, don't you?

LODGE: Brumby? *(looks* BRUMBY *over)* Why, of course. Lt. Brumby! The young man who went off to the war!

BRUMBY: Pleased to see you again, Senator.

ROOSEVELT: And this is Mrs. Brumby.

(EMILIE *remains seated, bows*)

LODGE: Well! How do you do? (*noticing* BRUMBY *is not in uniform*) Have you left the Navy, Lieutenant?

BRUMBY: (*smiling, a little embarrased*) It's . . . it's a long story, sir.

LODGE: Oh? Well how do you like the new arrangement? (*nudging him playfully*)

BRUMBY: Sir?

LODGE: I mean, when you were here last, your boss, Secretary Long, was also Mr. Roosevelt's boss. Now Mr. Roosevelt is Secretary Long's boss (*looking at* ROOSEVELT *proudly*), our boss! (*there's polite laughter*) And here you are—married to this charming young lady, and mmmm a little older perhaps.

BRUMBY: And I hope a little wiser, sir.

LODGE: Yes, Yes. Well I hope we all are (*turning to Roosevelt*). Theodore, I came about the Hepburn bill. It may have passed the House handily but I'm afraid it may have rough sailing in the Senate.

ROOSEVELT: Why should it?

LODGE: Theodore, most of the senators are for more stringent penalties against rebating by railroads. They are also for publicizing railroad earnings . . .

ROOSEVELT: But?

LODGE: But not all of them think the freight rates excessive. They don't favor regulation.

ROOSEVELT: Including you, Cabot?

LODGE: *(evading the question)* Now, Theodore. You are stepping on some very stubborn and important toes. You know Senator Aldrich, our party whip, is John D. Rockefeller's son-in-law. He and Senator Elkins are out to embarrass you. And Tillman of South Carolina—he favors regulation but he hasn't forgiven you yet for inviting that Negro Booker T. Washington to dinner at the White House!

ROOSEVELT: I thought the Civil War had settled all that!

LODGE: Theodore, sometimes to get farther we have to tread lightly, or, as you say, speak quietly while we carry a big stick!

ROOSEVELT: *(angrily)* No, Cabot! No!

I will shout quite loudly
And carry a giant stick:
And I will do it proudly—
These people make me sick!

CABOT: *(to* BRUMBY *and* EMILIE*)* That's true. They do make him sick!

BRUMBY: Who, sir?

ROOSEVELT: Who?
Those wealthy malefactors
With their sly arithmetic
Those revenue subtractors
Those people make me sick

LODGE: *(as* BRUMBY *and* EMILIE *show more interest)* Ah,
    yes, and . . .
    Those business houses rambling
    Who make their profits quick,
    Not by work but gambling—
    Those people make him sick!

BRUMBY: *(now getting into the spirit)* Bravo, sir . . .
    And what of raw material
    Which conquered people pick
    For industry imperial—
    Doesn't that *make you sick?*

LODGE: *(not liking the trend)* Later, boy later.

ROOSEVELT: (confusing the issue)
    Those mining bosses who will
    Unions try to lick
    Even if we're out of fuel—
    Those people make me sick!

BRUMBY: But, sir . . .

ROOSEVELT: *(ignoring the intervention)*
    Those railroad operators
    Who'll raise the price of tic-
    kets! Those freight rebaters!
    Those (growling at Lodge) *people make me sick!*

LODGE: A little patience, Theodore.

ROOSEVELT: Brumby, do you know the things I've been
    called in this fight for labor and against monopolies?
    Tyrant! Demoagogue! Why, I've been even called a
    liar! How can the President of the United States lie!

LODGE: Never!

ROOSEVELT: I've been fair and acted without favor in this whole thing. Why only last month a Federal Grand Jury in Kansas City accused of receiving or granting freight rebates such eminent Republican campaign contributors as the Armour Packing Company, Swift and Company, the Cudahy Packing Company, Nelson Morris and Company—as well as the Burlingame, the St. Paul, and the Chicago and Alton railroads! Did I raise a finger to stop it?

LODGE: No!

ROOSEVELT: Ah, but Brumby, I have my ultimate target—my foe *par excellence!*

LODGE: J.P. Morgan?

ROOSEVELT: No!

LODGE: Northern Securities?

ROOSEVELT: No!

(Sings. Tune is reprise of first scene song, in slower, more serious tempo.)

> *The battle I will carry*
> *Against an adversary*
> *Who's worthy of the Presidential foil!*
>   (fencing gesture)
> *I mean, of course, that giant*
> *So slimy and defiant*
> *That monster by the name of Standard Oil!*

LODGE: Aha! *(joins* ROOSEVELT *in duet)*

> *With Standard's rates so secret,*
> *As near as we can fig'r it,*

They're making millions yearly quite illegally!
Which doesn't pack the folders
Of many poor stockholders
But only a few who live their lives quite
*   regally!*
Yes, we are steadfast comrades
In battling those conglom'rates
Of companies whose tactics quite disgust us!
What's good for Standard Oil
Isn't good for those who toil
And who have waited long for social justice!

(At the end of the song, ROOSEVELT and LODGE look at BRUMBY and EMILIE, hoping to see them getting convinced.)

BRUMBY: *(mellower now but still somewhat dubious)* That is all fine, Mr. President. But . . . *(he looks at EMILIE and holds her hand)* we still cannot see what this has to do with justice for people ten thousand miles away.

ROOSEVELT: Don't you see, Brumby? *(gravely)* Before we can be just to others we have to be just to ourselves, to our own people. We have to show the world that our system can bring justice to all of us. And we can do it!

LODGE: Of course we can!

ROOSEVELT: There is a new destiny shaping up for us, Brumby, and I think it is this: If we solve the problem of justice openly, freely, publicly, using all the powerful means of communication at our command, so that all of America and all the world may see—if we keep the will to set ourselves aright—then we may yet truly claim the right to set the world aright. Then we may yet be the leaders in a world social revolution in freedom!

(ROOSEVELT *takes* EMILIE'S *hand and* LODGE *takes* BRUMBY'S.
With their hands thus locked, ROOSEVELT *begins to sing. As he
sings, he looks at* EMILIE, *then at* BRUMBY, *urging them to join.)*

> *There is no place in our world*
> *for nations meek as cattle*
> *Who hesitate to fly the burning standards into battle!*

(LODGE *has joined in and* BRUMBY now picks it up)

> *There is no race that can survive*
> *by standing soft and courteous*
> *While others pass it by in hot pursuit*
> *of fighting virtues!*

EMILIE:
> *It is possible*
> *After you've slapped your neighbor*
> *To offer him your hand.*

BRUMBY:
> *It is possible*
> *After you've knocked him down*
> *To pull him back to stand.*

BOTH:
> *It is possible*
> *To start doing just that*
> *Without asking why*
> *There is really*
> *Nothing we could lose*
> *If we try.*

COMPANY:
> *You may be skilled in battle or winning bloody glories,*
> *Or sinking helpless navies and seizing territories;*
> *But you'll never be a model for social revolution*

Unless you prove that freedom is a better institution!

Hail to every nation that is a conqueror,
But hail to her who conquers her selfishness before!

The will! The will! The will to go and fight!
The will! The will! to set ourselves aright!

THE END

BIBLIOGRAPHY
The following bibliography was used as background
in writing the play *Manifest Destiny*.)

Aguinaldo, Gen. Emilio and Pacis, Vincente Albano. *A Second Look at America*. New York: Robert Speller & Sons, Publishers, Inc., 1957.

Alfonso, Oscar M. *Theodore Roosevelt and the Philippines 1897–1909*. Quezon City: University of the Philippines Press, 1970.

Alzona, Encarnación. *Galicano Apacible, Profile of a Filipino Patriot*. Manila, 1971.

Angle, Paul M. *The Making of a World Power*. Greenwich, Conn.: Fawcett Publications, Inc., 1960.

Beale, Howard K. *Theodore Roosevelt and the Rise of America to World Power*. New York: Collier Books, Macmillan, Inc., 1968.

Blount, James H. *The American Occupation of the Philippines 1898–1912*. New York and London: G.P. Putnam's Sons, 1912.

Bryan, William Jennings, et al. *Republic or Empire? The Philippine Question*. Oakland, California: Occidental Publishing Company, 1899.

De la Costa, S.J., Horacio. *Readings in Philippine History*. Manila: Bookmark, 1965,

De Novo, John A. *Selected Readings in American History*. New York: Charles Scribner's Sons, 1969.

The Development of the Philippine Public School System. Manila: Bureau of Public Schools, 1966.

Dewey, George. *Autobiography of George Dewey, Admiral of the Navy*. New York: Charles Scribner's Sons, 1913.

Dulles, Foster Rhea. *America's Rise to World Power 1898–1954*. New York: Harper & Row Publishers, 1954.

Foner, Philip S. *The Spanish-Cuban-American War and the Birth of American Imperialism 1895–1902*. New York, London: Monthly Review Press, 1972.

Glad, Paul W. McKinley. *Bryan and the People*. Philadelphia, New York: J.B. Lippincott Company, 1964.

Hofstadter, Richard. *The American Political Tradition and the Men Who Made It*. New York: Robert Speller & Sons, Publishers, Inc., 1957.

Horrabin, James Francis. *An Atlas of Empire*. New York: Alfred A. Knopf, Inc., 1937.

Kipling, Rudyard. *Rudyard Kipling's Verse. Definitive Edition*. London: Hodder and Stoughton, Ltd., 1948.

Lininger, Clarence. *The Best War at the Time*. New York: Robert Speller & Sons, Publishers, Inc., 1964.

Majul, Cesar Adib. *The Political and Constitutional Ideas of the Philippine Revolution of 1896*. Quezon City: University of the Philippines Press, 1967.

Miller, Douglas T. *The Birth of Modern America 1820–1850*. Indianapolis: Pegasus, the Bobbs-Merrill Co., Inc., 1970.

Miller, Richard H., editor. *American Imperialism in 1898, The Quest for National Fulfillment*. New York: John Wiley and Sons, Inc., 1970.

O'Connor, Richard. *Pacific Destiny*. Boston: Little, Brown and Company, 1969.

Perkins, Dexter. *A History of the Monroe Doctrine*. Boston, Toronto: Little, Brown and Company, 1941.

Pringle, Henry F. *Theodore Roosevelt, A Biography*. New York: Harcourt, Brace, Jovanovich, Inc., 1932.

Revel, Jean-François. *Without Marx or Jesus, The New American Revolution Has Begun*. New York: Dell Publishing Co., Inc., 1972.

Schirmer, Daniel B. *Republic or Empire, American Resistance to the Philippine War*. Cambridge, Mass: Schenkman Publishing Co., Inc., 1972.

Schott, Joseph L. *The Ordeal of Samar*. Indianapolis, New York: The Bobbs-Merill Co. Inc., 1964.

Scott, John Anthony. *Living Documents in American History. No. 2*. New York: Washington Square Press, 1969.

Selections from the Correspondence of Theodore Roosevelt and Henry Cabot Lodge 1884–1918, Vols. I and II. New York, London: Charles Scribner's Sons, 1925.

Stickney, Joseph L. *Admiral Dewey at Manila.* Philadelphia: J.H. Moore Company, 1899.

Storey, Moorfield, and Lichauco, Marcial P. *The Conquest of the Philippines by the United States 1898–1925.* New York and London: G.P. Putnam's Sons and the Knickerbocker Press, 1926.

U. S. Political Pamphlets, Vol. 14. A collection of pamphlets on the Philippine questions 1901–1903, bound by the library of Cornell University.

Wolf, Leon. *Little Brown Brother.* New York: Doubleday & Company, Inc., 1961.